Homeland

Post Printing Notes for the Reader

The book went to press just prior to
Benjamin Netanyahu's successful re-election as
Israel's Prime Minister in 2008.

The dotted line on the maps found on the endpapers
indicates the route taken by the ship Draga 1.

Rabbi of Czor-ov should read Czortkov pages 5,14,16,
and index.

The words 'Valley Authority' should be omitted following
the word Jordan on pages xxiv and 30.

Dr. Hacohen passed away on 21 Adar Bet 5768, p.222.

תל חי

DR. MORDECAI HACOHEN

Homeland

From Clandestine Immigration to Israeli Independence

BEAUFORT
BOOKS

First Edition

Library of Congress Cataloging-in-Publication Data

Hacohen, Mordecai, 1919-2008
  Homeland : from clandestine immigration to Israeli independence / Mordecai Hacohen.
     p. cm.
  Includes index.
  ISBN 978-0-8253-0590-0 (alk. paper)
  1. Hacohen, Mordecai, 1919-2008 2. Jews—Austria—Vienna—Biography.
3. Jews, Austrian—srae—Biography. 4. Zionists—United States
Biography. 5. Vienna (Austria)--Biography. I. Title.

  DS135.A93H335 2008
  320.54095694092—dc22
  [B]
                              2008016931

Published in the United States by Beaufort Books, New York
www.beaufortbooks.com

Distributed by Midpoint Trade Books, New York
www.midpointtrade.com

Interior design by Elyse Strongin, Neuwirth & Associates, Inc.

10 9 8 7 6 5 4 3 2 1

Printed in the United States of America

Introduction

THE PUBLISHING of Dr. Mordecai Hacohen's memoirs could not have come at a better time. Today, 60 years after its birth, the State of Israel is under an unprecedented assault. While this assault comes in many forms—military, diplomatic, political, and economic—above all, it is moral in nature. The enemies of the Jews seek to undermine our belief in the justice of our cause. They know that a Jewish people shorn of this sense of justice will no longer have the will to defend itself.

MORDECAI HACOHEN was a man whose faith in his people and their rights never wavered. His life story is the story of the Jews' remarkable transformation from powerlessness to power. It is a story of the tragedies that befell us when we relied on others for our defense and the triumphs we realized when we were bold enough to determine our own future.

INSPIRED BY the powerful and prescient ideas of Ze'ev Jabotinsky, he joined the Betar movement and eventually made his way to Israel. As you will read in these pages, his contribution to the State of Israel and to the Jewish peo-

ple was broad and deep. He dedicated his life to safe-
guarding our rights and to strengthening a Jewish state he
so profoundly loved.

MORDECAI WAS a true Jewish patriot, and I am proud to
have called him a friend. May his memory be blessed and
may more of our people follow in his righteous path.

Benjamin Netanyahu
Former Israeli Prime Minister

Dedication

THIS BOOK is dedicated to my wife, Hoshanah Eliovson Hacohen, granddaughter of Rav Moshe Leib Bernstein, a founder of the Shaare Hessed neighborhood in Jerusalem, and Yehoshua Eliovson, a founder of the city of Tel Aviv, and to my children, their spouses and my grandchildren: Israel and Sandi Hacohen, Ariel Menahem Hacohen, Naomi Malka and Dr. Steven Weiss, and Yael Pnina and Neil Wasserman.

•

THESE MEMOIRS also pay homage to Vladimir Ze'ev Jabotinsky, tireless champion of the Jewish people, who saved my life, the life of my parents, and the lives of many thousands of Jews who heeded his message and took action to evacuate Europe and immigrate to the land of Israel. We are forever in his debt.

Vladimir Ze'ev Jabotinsky (1880–1940) was a gifted journalist, compelling orator, and dynamic Zionist leader. He had the clarity of vision to identify the mounting danger to European Jewry in the 1930s, the wisdom to address the crisis, and the courage to speak out urgently and warn Jews to "eliminate the diaspora" before "the diaspora eliminates you."

Notwithstanding vilification, imprisonment, and exile in pursuit of his mission, Jabotinsky energetically dedicated his life to rescuing Jews. These activities paralleled his efforts to achieve the restoration of an independent Jewish state in its national ancestral home in the land of Israel. His speeches and writings galvanized a generation to take risks and make sacrifices to realize Theodor Herzl's dream of Jewish statehood. Ze'ev Jabotinsky's teachings guided my life from childhood. May his example inspire future generations of Jewish leaders!

•

ONE HUNDRED and fifty three members of my family—men, women, and children, scholars, businessmen, and professionals—who lived in Poland and did not follow the path of Zionism, perished in the Holocaust. May the Almighty avenge their blood!

Dr. Mordecai Hacohen
Biographical Timeline

1919–1938
- Early Years in Vienna

1925
- Acquired an interest in following current events by reading the newspaper daily to his bedridden grandfather

1930
- Joined the Betar Youth Movement

1936
- Nominated by Otto Seidman, Netziv Betar of Austria to coordinate *Aliyah Bet* the Clandestine Immigration (Underground Railroad)

1938
- Set up kitchen for kosher food distribution to prisons
- Using press card got in to see French Consul to arrange release of his cousin from detention by Nazis
- Initial transport stopped at the Italian border

VOYAGE OF THE DRAGA I

1939–1950 Life in Eretz Israel
- Entrepreneur—supported self and parents by selling feathers and flowers to millinery shops and later textile remnants

1939
- Attended Hebrew University—active in Yavneh VeYodpat Student Organization

1945
- Produced and Narrated Radio series on the contribution of Viennese Jews to the Arts
- Attended concerts at the Jerusalem Y and at the Edison Theater
- Close friend to leading artists and musicians of the day—Tzvi Zeitlin, Alex Weissenberg, Ella Goldstein, and Leonard Bernstein
- Cousin of Abel Pann, internationally known artist and founder of the Bezalel Academy of Art.
- Regularly entertains at Café Atarah
- Administers and attends Jerusalem Tutorial Classes in Public Administration

GOVERNMENT STATISTICS
- Civil Guard during siege of Jerusalem
- Marc Aviezer
- Rescuing the Diplomatic Library
- Establishment of the Foreign Ministry
- Arrival of Russian Ambassador
- Arrival of American Ambassador

Preface

IN DESCRIBING my childhood and involvement in the youth movement in pre-war Vienna, my leading an "underground railroad" transport of Jews fleeing the Nazis to the land of Israel, and my role in the re-establishment of an independent Jewish state in Israel, I hope to provide an idea of the challenges we faced prior to having our country restored to us after two thousand years of exile. I expect you, the reader, to come away from my humble memoir with an enhanced appreciation of the groundwork performed, often behind the scenes, by people who were never headliners.

I will, in the process, be narrating events not necessarily well known even to historians, about individuals whose contributions deserve to be documented. I cannot stress strongly enough that, although I mention a number of well-known people—even celebrities— the independence movement and the progress of Israeli society was accomplished in large measure by anonymous individuals. I want to stress to the reader, that whatever your fame or lack of it, you too can contribute to the process of change, towards peace, security, and prosperity. I hope you chose to take up the challenge.

Contents

Prologue:
The Jabotinsky Dinner

ONE OF the highlights of my life of service to the State of Israel and to the Jewish people was at a dinner in 1980. On this occasion, shortly after his election as prime minister of Israel, Menachem Begin arrived in New York and was to be a distinguished guest at a special memorial dinner and tribute to Ze'ev Jabotinsky, which I undertook to organize. On previous occasions, when Begin was addressing leaders of the United Jewish Appeal or the Israel Bond Organization, I would introduce him to the audience. When I compared him to our mentor, Ze'ev Jabotinsky, Begin would shake his head in disagreement. He felt that no one should be compared to the greatness of Jabotinsky. The 1980 dinner was a gala salute to Jabotinsky, one of the most charismatic leaders and speakers of the twentieth century, on the centennial of his birth, where Begin and many other luminaries would be in attendance.

Begin arrived on El Al in New York, landing at a special section of Kennedy Airport. The Mayor of the City of New York, Abraham Beame, with whom I had coincidentally worked in the American Bank and Trust Company, and I received the prime minister and his entourage. Also present were Chaim Herzog, who later became president of

Israel; Eliahu Ben Elissar, Begin's close advisor; ambassador to the United States Simcha Dinitz; and Israel's Consul General in New York. I greeted Begin by pronouncing the Hebrew blessing *Shehechiyanu, v'kiy-manu v'higiyanu laz-man ha-zeh* (who sustained us and kept us to reach this day). I meant it as an expression of thanksgiving for his role in Israel's struggle for independence and to—what was then—his recent return to the political limelight. There was a time when Begin was treated virtually as a pariah, a hero left in the wilderness.

Those who officially welcomed him, accompanied by the FBI and the New York City Police Department, escorted the prime minister to the Waldorf Astoria Hotel, where I had arranged his accommodations in the presidential suite. The dinner was to be held in the Waldorf's grand ballroom and broadcast simultaneously to other ballrooms in the hotel to accommodate the anticipated overflow crowd.

Earlier in the year, I had been invited to join the Jabotinsky Foundation in organizing this Centennial Dinner and to be its co-chair. I marshaled my considerable experience in organization and contacts I had made in the course of my activist's life to make this an unforgettable event. It came to be regarded as the greatest Jewish event ever held in New York City. Over three thousand guests attended the black-tie affair. Included in the dinner committee would be all the diplomatic representatives of Israel in the United States; the U.S. ambassador to Israel; and four co-chairmen—Milton Petrie, Erik Spektor, John L. Loeb, Jr., a former U.S. ambassador to Denmark, and myself. Serving as honorary co-chairmen were twenty-one presidents of major Jewish organizations: thirty-five United States senators, twelve state governors, twenty-four congressmen and eight hundred members of the dinner committee. If this sounds like an overwhelming amount of planning, you will see in the following pages that my involvement in the establishment and survival of Israel dwarfs lesser organizational tasks. While planning an event of this magnitude was hardly routine, I was very comfortable with the level of detail and coordination required.

One visitor, Yaakov Meridor, my former commander in the Irgun Tzv'ai Leumi, was a proven hero in that capacity. Meridor had been injured while defending the city of Jerusalem in 1948. When Menachem Begin arrived in Eretz Israel, Meridor turned the leadership of the Irgun Tzv'ai Leumi, over to Begin. With his characteristic modesty, Meridor asked my permission before entering Begin's suite. The dinner was a joyous but heavy responsibility for me, and this was a heady and humbling not to mention, unnecessary, gesture on Meridor's part.

Thirty-two years before, in 1948, at a sumptuous dinner of the United Jewish Appeal following Israel's victory in the War of Independence, I had had a similar encounter with Meridor. When I arrived at the UJA's dinner, I saw Meridor standing in the hotel lobby. He asked me if I would be able to intervene and obtain an admission ticket for him as he had not been invited. I approached the executive vice president of the UJA, who was associated with the socialist Mapai (Laborites, a rival party) and complained about this oversight. Meridor was instrumental in the liberation of Israel from the British. In my opinion,

this slight was inappropriate and unquestionably intentional. Within minutes, Meridor was not only admitted
but was given a seat of honor at the dinner. At the
Jabotinsky dinner, then, I was able to do another yet
smaller favor for this hero in Israel's struggle.

To make this grand event an outstanding, well-
attended, funded, and publicized one, took more than a
year of preparation. I had gone to Hollywood, where
publicity is an industry in itself, and enlisted the participation of Sherry Lansing, then the president of Twentieth
Century Fox, as well as Danny Kaye and several other
celebrities. I also engaged the attendance and, in some
cases, the performances of Otto Preminger, Lee Strasberg,
Roberta Peters, and Jan Peerce from the Metropolitan
Opera in New York, and Misha Raitzin from the Bolshoi
in Moscow. Cantor Josef Malovani, Ellen Burstyn, and
Celeste Holm read selected writings from the works of
Ze'ev Jabotinsky. Introducing the artists was my friend
Martin Bookspan, commentator of the *New York Times*
radio stationWQXR in New York. A brilliant choir
including fifty cantors from various synagogues in New
York sang, under the direction of Seymour Silbermintz;
the Pirchei Yerushalayim choir performed "Hatikvah,"
the stirring national anthem of Israel and America's
anthem "The Star-Spangled Banner." The anthem of
Betar, the youth organization I had joined in Vienna, was
recited by the legendary Stella Adler, accompanied by the
U.S. Army Band under the direction of Michael R.
Mosher. I also arranged for a presentation of colors by
cadets from the U.S. Military Academy at West Point.
Joined by veterans of the Jewish Legion, Jewish war

veterans of the United States, the Shomrim Society (Jewish members of the New York City Police Department), and the honor guard of Betar, they provided a dramatic background to a taped historical oration by Jabotinsky.

So that the audience could hear Jabotinsky's actual voice, I obtained a recording of his address to the Peel Commission in London in 1936, in which he predicted the establishment of the Jewish state within ten years. It was necessary to improve the recording as it was difficult to follow his speech in the condition in which I found it, which I did with the help of the FBI's phonetic unit, located at Queens College in New York. Visiting there, I was received—and rather taken aback—by a Hassidic Jew with a long beard. For a moment it appeared as if I had mistakenly come to an orthodox synagogue rather than to the FBI. However, this Hassid headed that FBI department and proved to be enormously helpful to us. I later learned that this group, skilled in phonetic reconnaissance, had been enlisted to assist with the Warren Commission's investigation of the murder of President John F. Kennedy.

To fully ensure that all the guests understood Jabotinsky's speech, we additionally distributed its text to the guests, the way it is done at presidential addresses to satisfy the media. Our artist, Michael Schwartz, produced an outstandingly designed dinner journal, which was also given to the guests. Both sides of the stage were adorned with banner-sized photos of Zionist leaders Theodor Herzl and Ze'ev Jabotinsky. Since I had only small photos of them and needed enormous enlargements to fill the massive size of the hotel walls, I went to Times Square and researched the artists and designers whose works were displayed in gigantic billboard announcements of the movies and plays that were showing in nearby theaters. We contacted the individuals who were experts in the enlargement process that our photos required. One of these designers offered to blow up my tiny photographs so that they filled the walls of the grand ballroom at the Waldorf. The results provided a striking backdrop to this stellar event, a splendid pageant in commemoration of a brave and deeply influential figure in my life.

As stated above, I went to Hollywood to invite film personalities to the Centennial Dinner. I brought with me a letter of introduction to Ms. Sherry Lansing from Otto Preminger, a friend who, like me, was a native of Vienna. Preminger is the noted film director of *Anatomy of a Murder*, *Exodus*, and *Hello Dolly*! Ms. Lansing received me cordially in her office at Twentieth Century Fox and listened attentively at my description of Jabotinsky's personality and forceful role in the events leading up to Israeli nationhood. I explained why it was so important that someone of her stature participate as master of ceremonies at the dinner. I was frankly very doubtful whether she would accept my invitation, although I had every reason to think she would be perfect for it. She was gracious, powerful, and had clout on both coasts. After I finished my introductory comments regarding Jabotinsky and his exceptional persona to Ms. Lansing, recounting that he was the head of the first Jewish army in World War I (fighting with the Allies against the Turks), the founder of the Haganah (the Israeli armed forces), and arguably the foremost leader of the Jewish people in our times, she stood up from her chair, embraced me and kissed both my cheeks, affirming that she would be honored to accept my invitation.

Following my visit to Ms. Lansing, I visited the home of Danny Kaye in Beverly Hills, this time with my wife and younger daughter in tow. Kaye, born Daniel Kaminski, also listened courteously to my description of Jabotinsky's historic achievements and contributions to the Jewish people. After a tour of the extraordinary Chinese kitchen in his house, for which he was well known and more than a little proud, he gladly accepted my invitation to attend the Jabotinsky dinner.

Shortly before a related honors ceremony, the bestowal of the Jabotinsky Medals, separate from the dinner itself, I received a call from Senator Daniel Moynihan and then-Congressman Edward I. Koch expressing their regret that they would have to decline their awards because we had also selected the fundamentalist Christian (and politically conservative) Dr. Jerry Falwell to receive an award. They chose not to join his company. I was sorry to receive their decision, especially from Senator Moynihan, whom I always considered a great friend of Israel. I did not share his judgment in this case, and still do not.

When Mayor Beame, himself Jewish, invited many leaders of the Jewish community to a meeting at his office, to enlist their cooperation at the dinner, I was asked to attend. Upon entering the room, I was embraced by one of the participants, my dear old friend, Yitshaq Ben-Ami, a former leader of the Irgun, with whom I worked closely in the clandestine rescue effort. We both witnessed the German army's march into Vienna. We had not seen each other in forty-two years, and his presence closed the circle of my activities on behalf of Jews and of Eretz Israel, our home. My career spanned more than forty years during which time I bore witness to and participated in historic events that transformed our world.

I was privileged to introduce the Prime Minster, His Excellency Menachem Begin, a Nobel Peace Prize recipient. Later, sitting adjacent to Mr. Begin, I heard Sherry Lansing announce the next song of Jabotinsky (he was a lyricist too!) sung by Roberta Peters and called "The Land of Eretz Yisrael is Mine," the anthem of Betar, the organization I had been associated with since my childhood. Begin, too, had been a member and had been its leader in Poland. I whispered into Begin's ear that this was not really the true title of Jabotinsky's song. Its "real" title and Jabotinsky's words were, "The Jordan Valley Authority has two sides, and both belong to the Jewish people." I mentioned to Prime Minister Menachem Begin that had Ms. Lansing announced the real name of the song, it might have caused a diplomatic incident between Jordan and the United States. There were tears in Begin's eyes as he heard my aside framed by this inspiring, emotional anthem.

תל חי

PART 1

A Viennese Childhood

I am grateful to my parents for raising me to observe the orthodox Jewish tradition and with a tremendous love. My father, although he was a Hassid (a follower) of the Rabbi of Czor—ov, was also dedicated to the Zionist ideal, as many Hassidim were not. He followed the teachings of the founder of the Zionist movement, Dr. Theodor Herzl. My father, together with his like-minded friends, helped in the organization of and attended the first Zionist Congress in Basel in 1897. When Dr. Herzl passed away in Vienna in 1904, he was buried locally. After the establishment of the State of Israel, in accordance with his last will and testament, Herzl's body was later laid to rest on Mount Herzl in Jerusalem. My father and I attended the service in Jerusalem and soon thereafter changed and Hebraicized our name (as was in vogue) from Nussenbaum-Stock to Hacohen; the *H* standing for Herzl,[1]

---

[1] My father specifically chose to add the Hebrew "H," heh (in English, pronounced "Ha") to record for posterity our family's religious Zionist origins and ideals. In Hebrew, though, "Ha" stands also for the definite article "The," thus distinguishing our family from other Cohens.

and Cohen because my family belongs to the priestly tribe, Cohen, descendants of our biblical grandfather, Aaron— Moshe Rabeinu's (our greatest prophet, Moses') brother.

Being raised in a warm and traditional Jewish home contributed to my sense of worth as an individual, as a Jew, and to my later commitment to the establishment and maintenance of a Jewish homeland, which would become my life's work. Due primarily to my mother and my maternal grandfather I learned to read at a very young age. As was the custom in Vienna, children and their mothers would visit beautiful Viennese parks every afternoon. When I was still a toddler, my mother often took me to the Votif Park, close to the University of Vienna. On the way, she taught me how to read the signs over the various shops, which enabled me, even before I entered elementary school, to read without difficulty. We would also stroll through another beautiful Viennese park, the Kay Park, which was just across the street from my grandparents' home. In the middle of this park, the city, under the administration of the Social Democratic Party and its mayor, Karl Seitz, built a large pool for children called *Kinder Freibad,* which was where I learned to swim.

After my grandfather suffered an accident and was bedridden, I would stop by to read to him from a variety of daily newspapers. Our conversations during these readings stirred my youthful self (by this time, ten years old or so) toward an interest in current events. The talks allowed me a glimpse into the personal lives of family members. One visit also led to one of the more embarrassing moments of my childhood.

My grandfather was at home in bed, but sharp-witted

and able to conduct routines of life, which included religious observance. The harvest festival of Sukkot was approaching, and it is a custom for Jews to utilize four symbols of agricultural products to celebrate this holiday: a *lulav* (palm frond), myrtle and willow branches, and an *esrog* (a Mediterranean citrus fruit, a citron, like a very large lemon). I made it my business to secure these items from the synagogue for my grandfather's use, and, when I went to shul, I immediately spotted a *lulav* and *esrog* unattended on a table. I proceeded to bring these to my pleased grandfather to make a blessing.

How was I to know that the items I had appropriated were intended for the special use of the spiritual leader himself? I had taken the rabbi's property! Their absence was palpable at the Sukkot services, and when I returned the *lulav* and *esrog,* my guilt was established, resulting in a rare experience for me, the net product of which was a sore bottom.

Following my daily reading of the news, my grandfather and I discussed the issues of the day at what later occurred to me was a fairly high level of discourse. My grandfather, in effect, showed me how to read the news "between the lines." He taught me the importance of seeking several alternative sources of information so as not to be a slave to a single opinion. It is the German journalistic style to be detached, often indirect, and, of course, after Hitler's rise to power in 1933, deceitful and selective. My scrupulous and inferential reading, my grandfather's legacy, enabled me to foresee events. Thus I concluded before the fact that sooner or later Hitler would come to power and that what he predicted, however horrible, would be carried out by the German army and its ancillaries.

Beginning in 1933, I saw from the news, the deterioration of my people's status in Germany. Signs such as "Boycott This Jewish Store" being one example. Other examples were how Jews were aggressively being humiliated, being forced to march through the streets of Berlin with yellow stars on their suits. This was increasingly aggravated within the next few years, and I quickly recognized how susceptible Austria would be to this kind of hooliganism posing as government. Through my diligent attention to the news, I anticipated the annexation of Austria (the *Anschluss*) and its neighboring countries even before the German army began to occupy Eastern Europe, France, and Western European countries. I believed and feared Hitler's threats to destroy the Jewish people. I concluded that my family and friends—indeed, all Jews—should be prepared to leave anti-Semitic Austria, ostensibly my native country as soon as possible. Many Austrian Jews, not excluding my parents, (as was also the case in Germany) derided me as an alarmist and planned on continuing their normal lives in what I correctly perceived would not be a normal world.

On March 11, 1938, when the Nazis invaded and annexed Austria I went to my family and in extremely forceful terms (I was then nearly twenty years old and capable of very direct speech) told them to abandon their possessions and property and be ready to depart (in fact, to escape) the very next day. They turned me down, mocking me, claiming that so many Jews still lived and flourished in Germany. However, in the days following the *Anschluss* the Nazi SS seized my cousin Isidore (Richard) Herrup and forced him to kneel on the ground and clean the streets while pouring acid on his hands. Only then did his family realize that the time had unquestionably come to leave all their belongings and flee Austria. It was no longer a civilized country.

As our historic culture was being undermined, my parents' departure was enabled by my courageous Uncle Aaron Vardi (my mother's brother, a director of the Anglo-Palestine Bank in Tel Aviv, later known as Bank Leumi) who sent Certificates of Immigration to my family. When my uncle offered me a student certificate for the Hebrew University or the Technion in Haifa, I refused, saying that I would not come to the homeland of the Jewish people, indebted to the kind "permission" of the British occupiers; I would not recognize their authority over me or any of us. Instead, I accepted a position offered by the Betar movement in Austria, placing me in charge of orchestrating what we would come to call the "clandestine immigration" to what would ultimately become Israel. The Brits referred to this noble effort as "illegal" immigration. I will use the former appellation throughout this book. It is, after all, correct. I could never conceive the saving of lives Jewish or otherwise as illegal in any way. It was by this covert channel, rather than by British sanction, that I was to enter Eretz Israel later that year.

I **WAS** born in 1919 in Vienna, soon after World War I. Ironically, in American president Woodrow Wilson's remembered and oft-quoted words, "the war to end all wars." At the time of my birth, my parents had been married for eighteen years, and lived a comfortable life in the magnificent city of Vienna. We lived throughout most of my childhood in the same apartment where I was born, until we left Austria in 1938. It was at 43 Obere Donau Strasse, near a tributary of the Blue Danube, the river and city of Johann Strauss and his musical family. That music infiltrated my soul; I have been a lifelong lover of great music and have even dabbled at being a musician.

Being an only child, I was so attached to my mother that I refused the separation required to attend kindergarten. Of course, I was also devoted to my father, but he was busy as a correspondent in the mammoth textile company owned by his brother-in-law, Lippe Turkel and Sons. Lippe Turkel was my father's oldest sister's husband, and his wealth allowed my own immediate family a privileged life for a time.

When I was six, my parents enrolled me in the Talmud Torah, an orthodox elementary school in the second district of Vienna, known as Leopoldstadt. Our neighborhood had absorbed many Jews from Galicia in Poland, such as my parents, who immigrated during World War I. My parents preceded most of them, though, because my father had been in the shipping business and had visited Vienna regularly before the turn of the century. During the winter months my mother sent me to a *cheder*[2] after school at a synagogue located across the street. There, in a private apartment, a teacher by the name of Levi

---

[2] A Cheder is the traditional system of religious education for Jewish youth; the precursor of the yeshiva, which is a place of higher learning.

taught me and other children—mostly immigrants from Hungary—Chumash (Bible) from the perspective of Rashi, the exemplary medieval interpreter. On the way home from the cheder, in order to encourage my daily attendance, my mother bought me delicious Viennese pastry in a bakery named after its owner, Pomerantz. This tactic worked spectacularly, and I attended school diligently, slowed down only a little by the sacher tortes.

It was my usual practice upon entering the bakery to quietly lock the door behind me, a tactic intended to keep rival pastry-eaters from getting at my coveted confections. Indeed, my own pastry-eating skills were so striking that Pomerantz once offered me (through my mother) an opportunity for unlimited sweets so long as I would eat them in the window: a kind of living advertisement for his goods. I forget why my mother declined (I am sure I was in favor of the idea), but in the long run it was assuredly a decision made in my best interest.

Vienna, like my current home, New York, is a walker's city. Vienna was then a beautiful sparkling cosmopolitan city full of culture, music, dance, and good humor. It had opulent royal palaces, the famous Spanish riding school, wide boulevards, great arches, fountains, and monuments. It had endless beautiful parks and playgrounds including the Pratter and its imposing Ferris wheel. The great historian Carl Schorske has described the magnificence of fin-de-siècle Vienna in his book of that name, and my childhood followed the turn of the century by only two decades. The architecture was imposing, and included a royal opera house, magnificent concert halls, theaters, and a great university. It was the city of Strauss and Mozart, and the parks rang with music from the free concerts staged there.

The Vienna of my childhood was marked by an efficient streetcar system. The Blue Danube meandered through the archetypal European city, which was surrounded by the mountains and the world-famous Viennese Woods. It was a hub of advanced science and medicine; of luxurious hotels and municipal squares, and an abundance of pastry and chocolate shops and cafés, the *conditorei* for which the great world city was known. As my later travels confirmed, it was the most beautiful and versatile city in Europe.

I grew up with an extended family that consisted of my grandparents on my mother's side and their four children, my aunts and uncles. I never knew my paternal grandparents; they had died in Poland long before I was born. My father's brother and my cousins lived in the same district, close to our home. I was particularly close to my maternal first cousin, Richard Herrup.

WE ATTENDED religious services in a cozy apartment in the same building where we lived, where a Hassidic rabbi Israel Manson, a distant descendant of the Baal Shem Tov, the eighteenth-century mystic known as the founder of Hassidism, led a small congregation. There I celebrated my bar mitzvah in 1932, followed by a reception at our capacious apartment. My mother's brother, Aaron Rosenbaum Vardi, the banker referred to earlier and an author of several books, came all the way from Eretz Israel to attend. In the *stiebel* (an informal place of worship) where I prayed, a distant relative, Alter Fuchs Safran, exerted a great influence on my religious orientation. I remember him on the eve of his own bar mitzvah, standing on the dining table in his apartment so as to add height to his thirteen-year old stature, to don his *tefillin* (phylacteries, the wearing of which was a symbol of adulthood and reverence) for the first time. And, since, by virtue of his bar mitzvah, he was now a man, I took his counsel very seriously on matters both religious and personal.

Every Friday night in the winter I was seated at the Safran's family table. I was brought the sort of food from home , which I would refuse to eat there. However, at the Safrans, I enjoyed eating it. At his own bar mitzvah, Alter Fuchs Safran impressively delivered a five-hour discourse on a difficult Talmudic tractate. At a very young age he was considered an *Iluy* a prodigy, an outstanding scholar of the Bible and Talmud, and he was ordained as a rabbi at the age of twenty. When the famous Rabbi Rozin (the Rogoshover Rav in the city of Dwinsk, Lithuania), passed away, during a stay in a Vienna hospital, Rabbi Safran was chosen to be his successor. After the *Anschluss* he brought his parents and sister to his new home in Dwinsk. The rabbi and his family were all killed when the Nazis occupied Dwinsk. Before their deaths, the Nazis had rounded up the Jewish population of the city, consisting of some 10,000 human beings and asked for a volunteer to come forward to be executed so that the rest of the population could go free. Rabbi Alter Fuchs Safran volunteered. As soon as he was killed, the rest of the community stood around helplessly and were savagely murdered by the Nazis.

Alter Fuchs Safran was one among 153 members of

my family, including their children, who were killed by the Germans in Warsaw, Krakow, Lwow (Lemberg), and other cities. One of my cousins, known as Yekele, the rabbi in Domboroff, thanked the Almighty before his execution for letting him die *al kiddush Hashem* sanctifying the name of the Lord by giving up his life solely because of his Jewish faith.

My father's brother, Samuel Nussenbaum, was privileged to be the designated Torah-reader on *Shabbat* (Sabbath) and Jewish holidays at the synagogue of a renowned Hassidic rabbi, Israel Friedman of Czor—ov. I was very proud of my uncle when I heard him read from the Torah during my visits to the synagogue. While there, I particularly enjoyed the Hassidic songs, full of joy but hardly unaware of the historical plight of the Jewish people. This reinforced an inclination on my part toward Jewish orthodoxy, instilled by my parents and, in my thus far short life, by many others.

As a student at the Talmud Torah elementary school I joined the religious youth group Agudath Israel. I attended their meetings every Saturday afternoon and to the degree that I could understand them listened to discourses on the Bible by prominent leaders of the organization.

After I completed elementary school my parents enrolled me in the junior high school, the Chajesgymnasium, named after the Viennese Chief Rabbi, Zvi Perez Chajes. He was a great man, but his namesake school was not the right one for me. The Chajesgymnasium mandated the study of Hebrew as a requirement, and I was unhappy with my Hebrew teacher there. I attended the school for only one year. Indeed, he failed me in Hebrew. Had I remained in that school, I would have been required to repeat the class and thus would have lost a full school year. I was very embarrassed to flunk Hebrew, since I was the son of an outstanding Hebrew scholar. This teacher had the nerve to pull my father aside and inform him that I would never master the Hebrew language. Many years later I met this same teacher in front of a store in Mt. Carmel in Haifa. He addressed me in German, but I responded in what was then fluent Hebrew. At the conclusion of our conversation, I politely, but pointedly, reminded him of his prediction that I would never master the language. He had no way of knowing that I had, in the intervening years, studied Hebrew literature at the Hebrew University with the renowned Dr. Josef Klausner. My erstwhile school teacher was quite uncomfortable, and I enjoyed seeing him walking away shaking his head, no doubt rethinking his mistaken prediction.

When I enrolled in the Sperlgymnasium, in consideration of my difficulties at the Chajes school, my parents hired a private tutor who came to the house every weekend afternoon to teach me Hebrew (this time with greater success) and prepare me for my bar mitzvah. The teacher, an ardent Zionist, convinced me (with my cousin Richard's reinforcement) to leave the very orthodox B-Grupe, the Agudath Israel, and join the youth organization for high school students, known as the VZM (*Verband Zionistischer Mittelschuler*) with its much more fervent Zionist leanings. A few years later the VZM moved to a location where I attended weekly meetings on the history of Zionism. We would celebrate *Shabbat* in song and cultural activities.

Every year, on the anniversary of Theodor Herzl's

death, the group   marched with other Zionist youth
movements to his grave in Dobling, a district on the outskirts of Vienna. There came a point when I, now a member of Betar, marched with them and other Zionist youth
organizations, waving blue and white flags. We impressed
not only the Jewish bystanders but also the many gentile
Viennese who watched our dramatic parade. Being a
Cohen (a descendant of Aaron, the brother of Moses, as
described on page 6), according to custom I could not
enter the cemetery and had to watch the memorial from
outside the gates.

A sizeable percentage of Viennese Jews were religious
and belonged to one or another of the seventeen existing synagogues in the various districts of the city. On the first day
of Rosh Hashanah, one could see many thousands of Viennese Jews lined up for miles at the banks of the Canal near
my home, where they went for *Tashlich*, symbolically throwing their sins into the river and out to sea.

The Polish Synagogue in Vienna, situated in the district where I lived, was under the spiritual leadership of the
learned Rabbi Meirson. It was later completely destroyed
during the German occupation. I attended services there
every *Shabbat* and on Jewish holidays and especially
enjoyed the performance of its outstanding choir, in which
two of my cousins sang. When I applied to join the choir,
my voice was deemed not strong enough, and I was, to my
disappointment, turned down.

The Hassidim, I observed, served G-d with something
approaching ecstasy. The atmosphere at the Czor—over
rebbe's home remains vivid in my memory. His rectitude and
love of humanity were a fine example for his congregation,

and especially the students, as was his extraordinary knowledge of Torah. To be in his presence and listen to his chanted Hassidic melodies was an unforgettable spiritual experience. His popularity among Hassidim was later demonstrated when over 30,000 Viennese Jews attended his funeral. I recall that as a young boy, I climbed up a tree in front of his house to watch the procession.

I enjoyed an enchanting childhood, but things were not idyllic for Jews, nor had they ever been. By the time of my adolescence, Vienna and Austria generally had long been anti-Jewish, and even the occasional breaks in persecutions were short-lived, lukewarm, and ultimately meaningless. In 1782, Emperor Joseph II, of the Holy Roman Empire, had issued the Edict of Toleration. While it granted the Jews certain rights, it stopped short of allowing them to found a congregation and organize public worship. It was only in 1823 that Jews were able to design a temple for themselves, and even then it was with the condition that the building not be visible from the street, visible, that is, by non-Jewish Austrians.

I mention this because one Friday evening, when I was ten years old, I stood with my mother across the street from the synagogue, set back from the street as it had to have been at the time of its construction and dedication, per the Imperial "concession," to watch Rabbi Zvi Perez Chajes leave by the exit reserved especially for him. A few days later, he passed away, and I attended his funeral. The public schools in Vienna were closed that day. All the rabbis in the city marched behind his coffin; all the streetlights in the city were illuminated in tribute.

The Nazis and their sympathizers were already making

their presence known in Austria and its largest city, Vienna, by that time (1929), nine full years before the *Anschluss*. On one of our innocent daily visits to Votif Park, near the University of Vienna, a horrifying commotion occurred. Years before, when a Zionist Congress had taken place in the Konzerthaussaal nearby, the Nazis had violently demonstrated outside, an ominous foreshadowing of the gruesome events to come. On this occasion, ten years later when I was with my mother, as the ruckus began, she took me by the hand and said, "Let's get out of here." I looked around and saw what appeared to be someone falling from the windows of the second floor of the university building nearby. I later discovered that a Jewish student was literally *thrown* out of the school window by Nazi youth and their Austrian sympathizers. My mother, not wanting me to see that atrocity and, knowing of its precedents, immediately led me away across the street to a building adjacent to the Hotel de France, on the Ringstrasse. This was a very posh neighborhood, with a doorman at each building. One doorman did not permit us to enter a building—*his* building—where we sought to take refuge, so she quickly ran with me to the next street, although fearful to arouse any suspicion among the public or the authorities. We entered a grocery store where she bought some sweets and we stayed there until it was safe to return to the street. The store, I remember, was across from the house where Sigmund Freud lived, Berggasse No. 9, an ironic reminder of Vienna being the home of both civilization and its discontents.

My political education—both in school and on the streets of Vienna—co-existed with my religious training, not common at a time when those realms were often widely separated. One influence on my theological upbringing had been the renowned Chief Rabbi of Vienna, Zvi Perez Chajes, notwithstanding my experience with the school bearing his name. He was an ardent Zionist and an outstanding speaker. My mother's sister, Aunt Bronia, served as his secretary. Along with my mother, I attended many Friday night services at his synagogue in the Seitenstettengasse in Vienna. I was called upon during my high school days to lead the congregation in prayer at *mincha*, the traditional Saturday afternoon service.

There was yet another Hassidic rabbi who earned my admiration, Rabbi Heschel of Kopitshinitz, the Kopitshinitzer Rebbe. When my grandfather became bedridden for many years as a result of a head injury, my mother took me to the Grand Rabbi Heschel late at night to request his prayers for my grandfather's recovery. His son, Abraham Heschel, who succeeded him, visited my grandfather's bedside almost every day. Their modesty and singular devotion also remain enshrined in my memory.

During World War II, while living in Jerusalem, I was suddenly awakened in the middle of the night by one of his Hassidim who asked me to get dressed and immediately come with him to see Rabbi Heschel in the Hotel Babad in Jerusalem. The rabbi urgently wanted to speak to me. At that time, I was an officer in the government of Palestine responsible for licensing the importation of commodities under the control of the government's Department of Light Industries. When I arrived at the hotel, I found many Hassidim milling by his door, waiting to enter his room. Despite this crush, I was ushered in as soon as I arrived and the rabbi asked me to obtain an import license for certain merchandise that was needed by the *Vaad Hatzalah*, a committee for the rescue of European Jews, of which he was a leading member. As difficult as this was for me, I issued the license without asking approval from my British superiors. In later years, I often met the rabbi in New York, and, until his death in 1960, I remained one of his most ardent admirers.

On one of his many visits to Vienna, I was also privileged as a child to meet the Vizhnitzer Rebbe, Rabbi Hager. Close to our home was a Vizhnitzer *shtiebel*. Whenever the rabbi came to Vienna on his way to Karlsbad, the administrators arranged a meal in his honor on Friday night that was also attended by his three sons. As a young boy, I attended the festive meals in the *shtiebel* of the rebbe and also received remnants of his food, distributed by him as a token blessing. One of those sons now lives in Israel where he has built an enormous yeshiva[3] in B'nai Brak financed by a good friend, Yitzhak Kassirer of Antwerp, the prominent diamond dealer. Another son lives in Monsey, New York, a vibrant orthodox Jewish community one hour north of New York City. The administrator of this *shtiebel* was Leibele Dickman who was saved and brought to Israel on one of the transports of the clandestine immigration, the dramatic story of which I will describe shortly. Other cousins of mine were Hassidim of Rabbi Israel Friedman of Husyatan, another descendent of the Baal Shem Tov. I often met the Husyataner Rebbe during my summer vacations at the

---

[3] Yeshiva: a religious school of higher learning where the Talmud is studied.

Austrian spa Bad Hall, and accompanied him on his after-noon strolls in the beautiful garden there. Soon after I immigrated to Eretz Israel I met with him in Tel Aviv and prayed at his synagogue on Bialik Street in Tel Aviv, across from the house of Israel's poet laureate, Chaim Nachman Bialik. Rabbi Friedman's house was also surrounded by a beautiful garden. To listen to his prayers and songs, which I did as a very young man, was magically inspiring. The rabbi and I often used to walk together in Tel Aviv where he named and pointed out with his silver-crowned cane every flower that grew along the way. A few years later, during Israel's War of Independence, it was found that he decreed in his will that he be buried in Jerusalem. If that request could not be fulfilled, he preferred to be buried in the holy city of Safad, and if *that* alternative should prove impossible, he expressed his desire to be buried in the holy city of Tiberias. Due to the War of Independence, the first two alternatives could not be met at the time of his pass-ing, and the rabbi was therefore laid to rest in Tiberias, where the Rambam (Maimonides), and other Jewish sages are interred.

After my short-lived experience at the Chajesgymna-sium, my parents moved me back to a public junior high school, the Sperlgymnasium, in the vicinity of our home, where I was required to study classical Latin and French. The rudimentary knowledge I acquired in those languages unex-pectedly proved very helpful years later when I became a world traveler and emissary and needed a functional fluency in several languages. Among other reasons, I had to be in contact with journalists in various areas where the local languages or a common language were utilized.

I had a math instructor there, Herr Hueber, a relative of the leading Nazi Hermann Goering. Hueber's strictness being a goad to us, and given the Viennese propensity for practical jokes, my classmates and I perpetrated one on him. One day, as a gag, we temporarily stayed out of class. When the teacher arrived at the scheduled time, he was puzzled by our absence, and went looking for us. We had, however, hidden ourselves well. While he was searching for us, ultimately soliciting the principal for help, we quietly filed back into our classroom and seated ourselves as decorously and studiously as possible, as if we had been there all the while. When Hueber, this time accompanied by the principal, returned and opened the claasroom door, he was speechless. We feigned ignorance, indeed suggesting that perhaps, in a school building in which each floor was identical, he had mistakenly gone to the wrong level.

This, as a joke, was marginally more elaborate than a customary game we played of staring at a particular object, a nearby rooftop for example, and seeing how many others we could get to follow our lead and look up to wherever we were focusing, bewildering them because there appeared to be nothing there that would merit such attention. Perhaps I mention this to point out that I was a normal adolescent, a "regular" teenager, which makes some of the subsequent events of my young life even more remarkably surprising.

At the age of sixteen, I was hospitalized for several weeks with a blood infection. During my recovery, still needing some home care, I was registered in a new private school, the Internat, in Mauer, to which I commuted despite its having facilities for boarding. The Internat was situated in the middle of the famous Viennese Woods and it had, as one would expect, a breathtakingly scenic campus. Many of my colleagues came from highly privileged homes of the Austrian aristocracy, so the school provided an excellent education. The school was exclusive, and only eight Jews attended out of a total student body of three hundred. Our classrooms in the spring were out in the open, surrounded by trees. The school building had once been a castle inhabited by Austrian noblemen. As I recovered fully, I enjoyed the many sports facilities, indulging in tennis, soccer, and handball. For the study of chemistry and physics we were able to use specially equipped laboratories. Since we had our meals at school, my parents arranged for me to receive kosher food. Every day a rabbi from the neighboring town of Modling delivered a kosher lunch. While there, I received private guitar lessons from a music teacher as an extracurricular activity.

Whatever academic subjects were taught in the morning were repeated in the afternoon in so-called repetition classes. Tutors supervised our preparation for examinations the following day. We were required to dress in uniforms like cadets.

Despite what must sound like a rigid and inflexible curriculum, my lifelong appreciation and love of music were cultivated there. I remembered it fondly years later, when I lived in America and attended the concerts at Tanglewood in the lovely Berkshire Mountains of Massachusetts. My summer vacations were often spent in Voslau where our relatively well-off family, the Turkels had a villa, which they opened to us, with guests staying at nearby homes, and also, in Grabenweg, a sprawling 200-acre country farm with no livable accommodations but having, amidst the few conveniences, a matzo-making machine, hand-operated in the absence of electricity there. At Voslau my cousins and I organized beautiful garden parties, and we prayed in our own synagogue on the top floor of the villa. Our *Shabbat* services were attended by many members of our families who came to visit over the weekend. The attendance was so great, the overflow impossible to seat in the main chapel, that many worshipers were asked to pray in the corridors.

As I grew older my mother took me to Bad (Spa) Hall and Bad Ischl, both famous for their healing waters. In Bad Hall, I entered a music contest to guess the works that were conducted by the local Kur (Spa) Orchestra under the directions of famous conductor, Maestro Hummel. Despite an audience and competitors much older than I and very sophisticated in their appreciation of music, I won first prize, and I was given Mr. Hummel's book of memoirs as a souvenir. This prize was presented in front of the crowd of onlookers, and I was very proud to win that prize while still a young man.

The spa had a theater featuring nightly performances by Austrian playwrights. There I met one of the artists who enlisted me to perform in a comedy. After being introduced as the director's secretary in the play, all I had to say, and barely audibly, was the word "Nebbish." Despite this very brief and undistinguished speaking role, my mother was very proud of my artistic talent.

At Bad Ischl, located in Upper Austria, guests came to drink the Jod (mineral) water that was considered very healthy. This spa was visited by many famous artists and poets. Otto Preminger's brother, Ingo Preminger, had a house across the main park. Otto was the director of the famous Viennese theater. In America, years later, we became close friends.

My mother and I also spent time in Salzburg, where we attended the famous summer music festivals with an orchestra under the direction of Arturo Toscanini. I was privileged to meet the great conductor after one of those concerts. The festival hall, famous for its performance of *Faust,* was on part of a mountain that was cut into two halves. The celebrated theater *regisseur* and artist Max Reinhardt, created what was called the Faust Stadt by bifurcating the mountain and building almost an entire city on different parts of it.

Ever since I was little, my mother had taken me to the Vienna Burgtheater, the famous classical stage in Vienna. For some reason, I particularly remember seeing a play by the Austrian writer Johann Nestroy called *Zu Ebener Erde und im ersten Stock* (On the Ground Floor and the Floor above"). My mother gave me a subscription to the concerts in the Vienna Konzerthaussaal, where I heard the justly renowned Viennese Violinist, Fritz Kreisler, and the Russian pianist and composer Sergei Rachmaninoff. After he performed the latter's famous piano concerto, the audience applauded and demanded that as an encore he play his "Rondo." When he finished, the audience again demanded that he *re*-play the "Rondo." Finally, Rachmaninoff, a very tall man with long arms, turned toward the audience and in his Russian accent said, "Some people say that I am a great composer. Others say that I am a great pianist. But I know one thing, that if I had not played the 'Rondo,' I would have remained unknown."

My appreciation of classical music has been a lifetime source of pleasure. As happens when one studies history, one's eye catches elements in history that touch on one's other interests. I learned that in order to succeed in their professions in intolerant times many Jews—such as Gustav Mahler, the famous composer and director of the Imperial Opera—were forced to convert to Christianity, well before the advent of Hitler. The internationally famous conductor of the Vienna Philharmonic and Opera, Bruno Walter, whom I often saw in person, facetiously asked, when told to convert, what religion he should accept. Viennese Jews were patrons of the thriving arts and music for which the city was internationally known and respected. A preponderance of the audiences of opera, concerts and theater performances was Jewish. Great Jewish composers and musicians could be found in almost every aspect of the city's music from popular songs to classical music. Vienna also produced a great composer of Jewish liturgical music, Cantor Solomon Sulzer, who was a friend of Franz Schubert.

My childhood subscription to the theater and to music performances and concerts inspired me—at the age of sixteen—to write the lyrics for two plays that were performed in the Stephanie Theater in Vienna. One of these revues entitled "Off to Palestine" (*Horuck nach Palestina*), a reflection of my burgeoning Zionism. The other, written in Hebrew but performed in German, was translated into English as "In Blood and Fire Judah Fell, and In Blood and Fire Judah Will Rise." Sixty members of the Betar youth organization performed in these plays and sang in a large choir. The music was written by friends, Jura Gilgun and Siegfried Lichtblau. Our performances were reviewed in the newspapers including the official organ of the Revisionist Party in Prague, *Der Judenstaadt*. I mention this because that paper issued me a press card, which proved particularly helpful following the German invasion of Austria. When thousands of Jews lined up in front of the French Consulate and other foreign missions to obtain the visas required for their emigration, I had no difficulty, thanks to that press card, in gaining almost immediate access to that haven during a period of intense crisis.

While in its confines, I met the French ambassador, François Georges-Picot, who had negotiated the Sykes-Picot Treaty. The little knowledge of French that I had acquired in high school proved beneficial. The ambassador complained about the mass flight of Jews from Vienna, but issued a transit visa for my cousin Richard, which enabled him to leave for London via France on his way to America. Horribly, many people who lined up in front of the Consulate to apply for a French visa were arrested by the Nazis and sent to concentration camps.

Later, when I was active in organizing the clandestine immigration to Eretz Israel, that same press card enabled me to enter the northern railway station in Vienna, to reroute a transport of immigrants from Poland to Vienna *Sudbahnhof*, where they continued on to Fiume in northern Italy for embarkation in our ships (see Part Two). That group was led by Aaron Propes, at the time the head of the Betar in Poland (before Menachem Begin took over as his superior), which had a considerable membership; one hundred thousand boys and girls.

For brief weekend getaways my mother rented an apartment for us next door to a villa where the son of the

King of Egypt—later King Farouk—lived. As a teenager, I played tennis and a version of handball with the so-called Playboy Prince in the courtyard of the hotel, next to his beautiful Rolls Royce. I continued to observe events in Germany by reading periodicals and newspapers available at an ice cream parlor near my home. My interest in central European politics grew commensurately with the concentration of news about the area, and, with it, concerns were dramatically reinforced. Many of my childhood friends and schoolmates were of the Catholic faith, and they, too, were influenced by the Nazi ideology that took deep roots after the rise of Hitler in Germany in 1933. One of my closest friends was the son of Austria's poet laureate, Kurt Wildgans, a Catholic whose father had married a Jewish woman. They were thus made highly sensitive to matters about which not all Austrians cared for. On our walks home from school, he would ask me with genuine concern what my plans were for the future and whether I wanted to stay in Austria in light of the rise of Nazism that demanded that Jews leave the country. I responded that although I was a native of Vienna, I had never regarded Austria as my homeland and would have no difficulty leaving. I was, like most Jews, a stateless person. My parents, although Polish citizens, did not register me at birth at the Polish Consulate in Vienna. They did not hold Polish passports, nor did they obtain one for me. I felt that I was living in Austria as a guest, and always regarded Eretz Israel as my national homeland. I looked forward to the day when I would be able to immigrate to the land of Israel, Eretz Israel, the homeland of the Jewish people.

MANY AUSTRIAN Jews, who counted on their rights as veterans of the Austrian army or its civil service, were disappointed to learn with the changing times that their citizenship did not protect them at all. The first responsibility of government is to defend its citizens, but that obligation did not, in the opinion of Austria's leaders, apply to them in Hitler's Europe. Considered subhuman, Jews would never be extended rights as citizens in Nazi-controlled territory. Reliance on Austrian justice was a reckless pipe dream, although one which many Jews adhered to until the end.

The castle that housed the Internat School may have been *too* attractive. When the Nazis invaded Austria, the bodyguards of Adolf Hitler were assigned to be stationed there. Dressed in their SS uniforms, replete with swastikas, they each wore an armband on his sleeve reading Adolf Hitler *Leibstandarte* (Adolf Hitler Bodyguard). At meals they sat behind my table, and would clearly have noticed that I was the only one in the area who was served a different menu for lunch every day. When my dangerously unsympathetic colleagues told them that I ate only kosher food, they kept surprisingly quiet, surely suppressing their instinctive contempt for Jews and things Jewish. In contrast, a Jewish classmate dyed his hair blond (i.e., Aryan) and wore a swastika on the lapel of his suit to hide his ethnic identity and try to gain favor with the Nazis. One day, because of that objectionable behavior, he was taken out to the garden of the school by the proto-Nazi thugs and forced to eat insects. This lesson might have taught him to respect his Jewish identity. It surely taught *me* that I had no choice but to bear mine proudly. That Jewish pride constituted a strong element of the integral dignity associated with Betar's Zionism, which I incorporated into my maturing personality.

I had an excellent teacher at the Sperlgymnasium, Professor Philip Roth, who inspired my lifelong interest in geography. At this writing, I am still an honorary member of the National Geographic Society of the United States. When I was able to visit most countries on the globe, I always remembered the lessons in geography that my teacher had illustrated with pictures and films.

From him, I learned about the Tennessee Valley Authority far away in the United States. The description of this unique project, using the river's power to generate electricity and, coincidentally, to provide jobs served as an example to me, something which I hoped to emulate some day in Israel. I thought that a TVA on the Jordan Valley Authority or on a potential Dead Sea-Mediterranean canal (the so-called Lowdermilk Plan) could produce electricity for the industrialization of the Negev, Israel's arid southern region, and could also irrigate a large part of other regions in the land. Such a canal would necessarily flow from the Mediterranean down to the Dead Sea's lower elevation (the world's lowest) and the steep descent would generate water power to drive electrical engines.

While the TVA was designed to control the vast abundance of water from the contributing rivers, Israel's problem was just the opposite—a serious shortage of water. I pursued my research for the implementation of this project throughout my academic career. Once I was in America, I wrote my doctoral dissertation at New York's prestigious New School for Social Research on this subject, and much of my life was devoted to pursuing the implementation of a multi-purpose project providing jobs, irrigation, and power. It would further provide a method of desalinization, which our country (and others) needed desperately. Although this project is revived periodically, it has never seen full fruition because of constraints on the Israeli budget, which by necessity must prioritize defense and security matters, and due to the usual Israeli political infighting.

I sincerely believe, and many scholars concur, that the interest of the Austrian people in the Nazi movement was deeply rooted in longstanding anti-Semitic attitudes rather than to anything new to the twentieth century. Anti-Semitism had historically been prevalent in Austria, sometimes with ironic consequences, one innocuous example of which I witnessed around this time, albeit virtually *in absentia*. Prior to the *Anschluss,* during the visit of Cardinal Innitzer of Vienna to my school, the Sperlgynasium, all the Jewish students were commanded to leave the school building. I joined my colleagues as we assembled across the street to observe Innitzer's arrival. Since the majority of the students at the school were Jewish, the Cardinal was shown what had, in our absence, become nearly empty classrooms. Innitzer, by the way, would welcome Hitler with open arms when he annexed the Cardinal's native land.

I had many gentile classmates who were Nazis. In daily discussions on our way home from school, they were hesitant to admit their affiliation with the Hitler Youth, which was outlawed in Austria at that time. They claimed only to be members of German sports clubs but I knew they were lying. I also saw the insidiousness of their charade.

As I grew into young adulthood in the 1930s, I noticed that protests against Nazi brutalities at the university and elsewhere, were sadly unavailing. A delegation from the Jewish Community Council in Vienna, the *Kultursgemeinde*, appealed to the Austrian parliament in protest against the chronic Nazi attacks on Jewish students. While the excesses continued unabated, and the police did not intervene, there came a day when a group of young Jewish boys lined up along the driveway leading to the main entrance of the university and pummeled every student who came out wearing a swastika on his lapel, a symbol of membership in or at least strong sympathy with the Hitler Youth.

Going back for centuries, the Viennese police had not been allowed to enter the grounds of the university, which were considered academic territory and therefore, in a civilized city, sacrosanct. A week after the "incident" when the Jewish youth attacked the swastika-bearing students the law was changed suddenly, and the police were allowed to enter the aula, the entrance hall to the university. This was presumably to keep order but in fact to repress Jews. This was a very significant and troublesome development and a manifestation of the further erosion of human rights in central Europe. On the other hand, having read this account in the newspaper I regularly read to my grandfather, I was inspired by the bold actions taken by these courageous Jewish youth, who were described in the report as "uniformed," and by the simple fact that their actions made a difference. It most likely saved my life.

OUT OF admiration, I was curious to know who the young boys were who attacked the swastika-bearing ruffians and was told that they belonged to a Zionist youth organization, Brit Josef Trumpeldor, named after a legendary Jewish hero. In 1930, tall and strong for my age, and wanting to assist in their efforts, I decided to join the group. My parents had no objection to my enlisting in Brit Josef Trumpeldor, known as Betar, the youth movement of the Zionist Revisionist Organization, which was truly a life-altering commitment.

With a stick in my hand and two belts around my waist, looking in my opinion very militant, I went to the headquarters of Betar and joined the organization. I have never left. The older Betarim were impressed by my sincerity, enthusiam, and determination, and I was admitted as a member of Betar's Junior League, Nesharim Eagles. On completion of a four-week course given by senior commanders of Betar, I received the first yellow stripes on my uniform, brown in color, designed to resemble the color of the earth of Israel. I was ten years old. When I joined Betar, it was already an international youth movement. In Vienna alone we had anywhere from 1,500 to 1,900 members, and I have mentioned the Polish rolls listing one hundred thousand youngsters. We had branches throughout Europe. The Betar in Vienna organized summer camps in Velden, Carinthia, one of the confederated southern states in the Republic of Austria, adjacent to the two beautiful lakes, the Wolfgangsee and the Keutschersee. It was there that I received my paramilitary training including fencing, calisthenics, and trench-digging in the hot midday sun. Less physically demanding were courses in Morse Code, map-reading, and other military disciplines. Required for the granting of my yellow stripes for leadership, these were the foundation of my activist and military life. In 1936, when I was called upon to help organize the clandestine immigration to Israel, I gratefully appreciated how helpful that training had been.

Attending these training courses in the following years, additional stripes were added to my uniform, and I was promoted to the rank of instructor. Upon my return to Vienna from training, I proudly displayed this distinction that was now visible on my uniform.

Most young people who identified themselves with Ze'ev Jabotinsky, Betar's leader, were members of Jewish student fraternities, the *Erbindungen*. They had been amongst the first to hail Jabotinsky, since their orientation was to defend Jewish honor. These members of student fraternities, with their colored caps and colored ribbons, had considerable influence on my younger age group, who looked up to them as what are today called role models, and Betar's enrollment grew, and so did our influence.

Betar was still led by Ze'ev Jabotinsky. His words and thoughts ignited idealism and enthusiasm that permeated the organization, and his vision instilled a pride and confidence in Jews young and old. Indeed, the foundation of Jabotinsky's brand of Zionism was a self-esteem that overrode years of oppression and, it must be said, Jewish self-denigration. Jabotinsky's message was that the lack of pride fostered cowardice and would lead to eventual and, by the 1930s, imminent defeat. That was the exact opposite of Betar's attitude.

My most dire apprehensions about the developing situation in Europe, however, were sadly confirmed not only by

Jabotinsky but by other Zionist leaders who visited Vienna—Chaim Weizmann, Nachum Sokolov, and others— and by lectures and readings by outstanding poets like Chaim Nachman Bialik and Shalom Asch who often came to Vienna and spoke at the Konzerthaussaal, always attended by a capacity audience.

Jabotinsky was an outstanding orator in German, one of the eight languages in which he was fluent. His knowledge of languages was so remarkable that once, during the visit to the president of Czechoslovakia, Jan Mazaryk, Mazaryk asked him in what language he preferred to converse. Jabotinsky responded that it was up to President Mazaryk to choose any language of culture he wished.

Weeks before his arrival in Vienna, notices on public bulletin boards simply announced, "Jabotinsky Speaks," indicating the date and place underneath. Having learned about Jabotinsky, the first soldier of Judah, the first Jew who formed the Haganah defense force in Eretz Israel, the founder of the Jewish Legion, the first Jewish army in 2,000 years, I awaited his appearances enthusiastically. To me, he represented the epitome of Jewish pride, a characteristic that had regrettably lessened with Jews' growing assimilation and make-no-waves attitudes. He told the Jewish people not to be cowards and not to be afraid, but to defend themselves. Jabotinsky preached that Jews, when united, were invincible.

Although many young people listened to Jabotinsky's speeches in Vienna, much of the audience was composed of older and successful men who were stirred by his words and manner of expressing them, but who often did not fully agree with him. Religious Jews particularly abhorred violence and challenged the ability of the Jewish people to resist aggression. They felt that resistance would only increase the danger of anti-Semitism. They were against the use of force even in self-defense. Many younger people, however, other than those assimilated and influenced by the powerful Socialist movement in Austria, followed Jabotinsky and felt that he was right to advocate Jewish resistance and reject the New Testament's "turn the other cheek" attitude when attacked.

The Jabotinsky movement, spearheaded the battle for restoration of Jewish sovereignty in the ancient Jewish homeland. His has always been a movement of ideas and ideals; of vision and dreams. It dreamt of Jewish statehood when others were afraid to define and pronounce that goal. It initiated Jewish self-defense and was wrongly labeled "militarist." Jabotinsky warned our people of the impending Holocaust long before the outbreak of World War II, when up until the declarations of war, Jews were still being told that "it can never happen." Jabotinsky pleaded for a mass exodus from Europe while members of his movement were called "panic makers." The Jabotinsky movement, implemented and conducted the largest rescue operation in our people's history when it was labeled "illegal immigration" by the British. It planned on the establishment of the State of Israel, and institutions such as a navy, before statehood loomed on the horizon. Jabotinsky, the idealist, was ironically, also, maybe foremost, a practical man, in some ways the quintessential pragmatist. His prescience seems even more remarkable in hindsight. The very idea of "a Jewish navy," for example, could not be grasped by many opponents, certainly not before the establishment of a Jewish state.

Belying the perceived total separation of Zionists and "religious" Jews, Jabotinsky was appreciative of religious practice, although he himself was not observant. He showed great respect for the observance of Jewish religious traditions and felt that the Jewish people's right to settle in Eretz Israel was based primarily on the commandments in the Torah. He was in turn respected by Jewish religious leaders and maintained a friendship with the world president of the Agudath Israel, Jacob Rosenheim.

Jabotinsky had decided at the Zionist Congress in Prague in 1933 to form the New Zionist Organization. He enlisted the support of Jewish organizations and invited them to be represented at its First Congress in Vienna in 1935. I was sixteen years old when this Congress was held in the *Konzerthaussaal* in Vienna. As an officer in Betar, I was assigned the role of an usher and worked around the clock, feeling that it was a rewarding experience if only to attend the meetings and listen to Jabotinsky's speeches. The Zionists of America were represented at that meeting by Jacob de Haas, a friend of Theodor Herzl and a member of the seminal First Zionist Congress in Basel in 1897, which my father attended as well. The Congress of the New Zionist Organization in 1935 was a similarly epochal event. Among the many personalities present were the British Colonel Patterson, Jabotinsky's commanding officer in the Jewish Legion during World War I. Another delegate on the dais was Dr. Isaac Alkalay, former chief rabbi of Yugoslavia and a prominent Sephardic leader.

The Konzerthaussaal was filled to capacity by an audience of 2,000 people. The highlight of the evening was an address by Jabotinsky, one of the most outstanding speeches I had ever heard. He analyzed the international situation and predicted the fate of European Jews. He concluded that European Jewry, not to mince words, was doomed. He spoke about the Jewish future in the most alarming terms. He maintained that we were entering a period that our tradition described as Messianic sufferings (*Chevlei Moshiach*). He said the contemporary Zionist leaders were political zeroes and completely unprepared for events that would soon occur. He warned Jews to pack their bags and leave Europe, and emphasized that the hour was five minutes to midnight. He called on Jews to leave Germany and Austria today, because tomorrow would be too late. Addressing himself to the Jewish masses of Poland, he also called on them to leave at once and reiterated his warning at a Revisionist conference in Warsaw adding: "Either you will liquidate the diaspora or the diaspora will liquidate you."

I took Jabotinsky's warnings very seriously, and adopted them, especially when he referred to Messianic sufferings. He predicted a catastrophe, cataclysmic in nature, unprecedented in Jewish history, and I feared something very much like that. I vividly remember the manner and the tone of his prophetic warnings. The only question I asked myself was a practical one: How we could prepare for the mass exodus from Europe? The British had closed the gates to Palestine. Immigration was curtailed to a fraction of what it had been, and there was no way one could legally enter Eretz Israel. Few paid attention to Jabotinsky's timely warnings. Some even spread the word that Jabotinsky was unnecessarily causing panic in the Jewish streets.

Sometimes it is difficult for Jews to remain united; indeed, when issues of life and death are not involved, it is almost an in-joke among us. It had been a sad moment, therefore, when an original participant, Meir Grossman, decided to form his own splinter party, the Judenstaatspartei, and left Jabotinsky's Revisionist Movement. Grossman was joined by Robert Stricker, vice president of the Viennese Jewish Community Council, and president of the Revisionist Zionists in Vienna. Robert Stricker later went to Paris, and when he came back after the Nazis invaded Austria, was sent to Dachau where he was killed. Betar, the fruit of Jabotinsky's evolution as an activist, was extremely well organized and structured, highly methodical, another legacy of its founder. Although Jabotinsky's own personal style was pre-eminently that of an artist and writer/speaker, his genius included not only dreams but the procedures for implementing them. He was a *true* visionary. Betar instituted goal-oriented systems and ways of reaching its objectives. We held weekly meetings, classes, cultural, and entertaining activities; parades with meticulously maintained uniforms, colorful flags, marching bands, and an anthem, composed by Jabotinsky himself. The pageantry of the Centennial Dinner in 1980 replicated the theatricality that was so much a part of Jabotinsky's character, and, not coincidentally, my own, as was my methodical approach to my work.

Betar's expressed goal was the Jewish return to our ancient homeland and to its former glory. This was couched in historic terms and rooted in the redeveloping dignity of the Jewish people. Our people have since learned that oppression can otherwise breed feelings of inferiority in the victims, thus perpetuating their victimization. My experience in the movement, combined with the Jewish values filling my home, were the basis of my adult traits of personal and Jewish pride (sometimes, it must be admitted, with brazen assertiveness) and a confidence to confront goals and hindrances straightforwardly.

During one of Ze'ev Jabotinsky's visits to our headquarters, I was honored and correspondingly proud to meet him. After he had finished his speech at a meeting of the Zionist Revisionist Organization, I approached him, saluted, and asked for his autograph. He signed his name, but added the Hebrew word "*aval*," meaning "but," signifying that it was not fitting for a member of Betar to request an autograph from him, as if Jabotinsky was an actor in the theater. I was teased by the seniors for having had the impertinence to approach Jabotinsky for his autograph. I was still undergoing my trial period in the movement and this was very upsetting. When I embarrassedly told my father about this incident and how chastened I was to have transgressed protocol, my father consoled me, saying, "You received more than you asked Jabotinsky. When he added another word to his name, it proved that Jabotinsky actually addressed you in person."

I had another opportunity to meet Jabotinsky shortly thereafter, following another of his lectures. I attended, by the way, *all* of his lectures delivered in Vienna and the surrounding area. That day, he left the building of the Revisionist Party in Vienna, late in the evening, accompanied by Naomi Weisel, the wife of a Revisionist leader in Vienna, Dr. Wolfgang von Weisel. Jabotinsky was returning to his hotel, the Continental, a fifteen-minute walk away. When he saw me in my uniform, he asked if I would accompany him. I was honored, told him so, and went along. However, full of my teenaged self-importance, I soon noticed my mother on the other side of the street, walking in the same direction and watching us along the dark Vienna streets. When we reached the hotel, my mother came forward to greet Jabotinsky, startling him and embarrassing me. He disingenuously asked me who this lovely lady was. I responded, a little awkwardly, that she was my mother. Jabotinsky complimented her on her maternal instincts and remarked that I was the very best member of Betar. When I mentioned Jabotinsky's compliment to my friends in the movement, they again ribbed me about my adolescent pride. I endured their teasing, even if benign remarks, for what seemed like a long time.

In the few months before the *Anschluss,* there were daily demonstrations in the streets of Vienna. On one side of the street marched members of the anti-Nazi Austrian Patriotic Front—demonstrating for the independence of their native country from German interference—while on the other side of the street pro-Nazi hoards were marching and shouting, "Heil Hitler." When it became abundantly clear that Germany's invasion of Austria was imminent, we instructed all the commanders of Betar units to be on the alert and that they were to proceed to their offices to rescue the incriminating blue and white flag of Betar and remove all of the membership cards when the invasion came.

After leaving synagogue on Friday night, March 11, 1938, I heard that Kurt von Schuschnigg, Hitler's proxy as Chancellor of Austria, had resigned, giving way to the German invasion that was about to begin. Following orders, I immediately proceeded to our clubhouse to remove our flag, which I wrapped around my body and took the membership cards out with me. The walk to my house ordinarily took no more than fifteen minutes, but with the flag around my body and the register of names in my hands, it felt as if this walk took a lifetime. As it developed, all the flags of the seventeen clubhouses of Betar in Vienna were brought to Israel intact. They are now displayed in the museum commemorating the immigration, a touching sight and a testimony to Betar's organizational efficiency.

Afterwards, many Jews were taken off the street and imprisoned in Viennese detention centers. The Passover holidays were approaching and posed the additional challenge of providing the families of the detainees with Kosher-for-Passover provisions. Betar decided to render what help it could. A leader of the Agudath Israel in Vienna, Wolf Pappenheim, obtained permission from the police to supply kosher food to the Jewish prisoners. A group of Viennese members of Betar volunteered to reopen a Jewish soup kitchen called the "*Einheit.*" With a colleague of mine, Yoka Fischbach, I traveled daily on a small motorcycle (with me sitting on the back seat) to raise money for the maintenance of this kitchen. It was long before the American Israel Distribution Committee had opened its facilities.

Going to to the detention centers for the actual food drops was an inherently risky maneuver. I hired a Viennese taxi with an Aryan driver visibly displaying a swastika on his car. When we reached the largest prison in Vienna (the *Landesgericht*), our first stop, the guards opened its huge gates and allowed the taxi to drive in. After we passed the first gate, another gate opened, but only after the first gate behind us was closed. Driving through the courtyard to the prison kitchen, I noticed detainees in their civilian attire, desperately and aimlessly walking around the prison yard.

By allowing us to deliver our Passover food, the Nazis spared themselves the cost and labor of feeding their prisoners. Upon unloading our food in the prison kitchen, we again passed through opening and closing gates. Every day of the week-long celebration, I delivered a supply of Passover food to inmates in seventeen prisons throughout Vienna. The last prison on my route was the youth prison, the *Jugendgefängnis*, where Jewish youngsters who had arbitrarily been rounded up were now incarcerated. Our supply of Passover food illustrated to the Jewish prisoners that we on the outside had not forgotten them and cared deeply for them. It was thanks to the Betar movement that the soup kitchen was opened and served its philanthropic (but very personally touching) purpose.

תל חי

PART 2

Father, I am Here

The Clandestine Immigration to Eretz Israel

One of the proudest chapters in my life was my role in the so-called clandestine immigration to Eretz Israel. In that campaign, we saved 26,449 Jews before, during, and after World War II. Britain had bolted shut the gates to Eretz Israel to Jewish immigration, cold-bloodedly rendering the escape of European Jews virtually impossible, thereby sentencing them to extermination. The Zionist Revisionist movement always claimed the right of the Jewish people to immigrate freely into the only Jewish homeland. Logically speaking, Jabotinsky asked: "Does an Englishman need a visa to enter England; does an American need a visa to enter the United States? Why should Jews require permission from England to enter their historic homeland?"

In reaction to the rise of anti-Semitism, the Zionist movement in Vienna became more active and broadly involved in the rescue effort. At Jabotinsky's urging, the Betar and Irgun Tzv'ai Leumi established two maritime schools for the training of Jewish naval officers. One was in Civitavecchia, north of Rome, where a ship purchased by Betar, called *Sara*,[4] named after the Jewish heroine, Sara Aronson was docked. Another school was established in Riga, Latvia, where another boat bought by Betar, the *Theodor Herzl*, stood anchored in its fine harbor.

We did not announce that these schools had any purpose other than to train Jewish sailors for a future Jewish state, in itself a controversial matter. No one was told that it was secretly a visionary project to facilitate the immediate immigration of European Jews into Eretz Israel surreptitiously. Jabotinsky's basic idea was to train Jewish sailors in the art of navigation so that they would be able either to navigate themselves or supervise the navigation of the ships of the clandestine immigration. Doing so would avoid the possible misdirection of these ships by those not directly involved in our efforts, but rather foreign crews working for hire. At the very least, they would be monitors, but theoretically they could serve as sailors, even captains.

Jabotinsky's idea to train Jewish naval cadets was rooted in his vision of breaking the British blockade of Eretz Israel. The future showed how farsighted Jabotinsky was in establishing these schools, because these naval officers were vitally instrumental in assuring that the ships navigated by Greek sailors were really headed for Eretz Israel. If our naval cadets had not been

---

[4] The leader of a spy ring supporting the British from within Ottoman-ruled Galilee a generation earlier, during World War I. She was motivated to defeat the Ottoman Turks largely because she had been an eyewitness to their genocide of the Armenians and feared a similar fate to those Jews under Ottoman rule.

standing near the compass in the command room of these boats to ensure that the Greek crew and the Greek officers led the ship in the right direction, we would have run the risk of exposing its human cargo to untold dangers. I commanded the first fully-loaded ship, the *Draga I*, and witnessed this extraordinary role of the young cadets. Of course, the trained navy would later be a component of the new Jewish state's essential military arm, thus their training was of double benefit. Jabotinsky exposed himself to criticism for training a Jewish navy prematurely, but that was only a secondary objective, and he endured the criticism.

Ze'ev Jabotinsky's idea of establishing these maritime schools was ridiculed by many Jews, like so many of his other prescient statements and warnings. Ignorant opponents commented that it made no sense to train naval officers as long as Jews had no sovereign state of their own, and thus neither an army nor a navy. What was the purpose of training seamen for an Israeli navy that was not in existence, indeed, had no ships? Jabotinsky foresaw the dawning establishment of a Jewish state, and, with the Haganah (the indigenous Israeli military in British Palestine) and this inchoate naval force, Israel would have, as would be eminently necessary, an instant military.

Ironically, Italy, under Mussolini's leadership, was sympathetic to the Zionist idea. Why? Because it opposed British policy. The Italians therefore constructed no obstacles, physical or governmental, to the establishment of the maritime school in Civitavecchia. The commander of that naval school was Yermiahu Halperin, a member of the high command of Betar, and a descendant of a famous family that was associated with the Shomrim Society in Eretz Israel. I knew Halperin to be an exemplary soldier. Physically, he resembled General Douglas MacArthur, and in terms of bearing and knowledge could have fit the part of an American commander or superintendent of an American military academy such as West Point or Annapolis. Halperin was the instructor of our First Officers School of the Austrian Betar. A native of Eretz Israel, he had two outstanding assistants: Mr. Baruch Blankenfeld, a lawyer in Jerusalem, and Mr. Josef Duckler. These assistants later conducted the officers' training school of the Betar, incidentally the inspiration behind the establishment of a branch of the Betar in Czechoslovakia.

We experienced no difficulty in recruiting volunteers for either of these schools in Italy and Latvia. The cadets, young high school students, came from cities in Austria, Czechoslovakia, Poland, Lithuania, Hungary, and Romania. Those who could not afford to pay for their own participation were subsidized by the Betar budget that was funded in part by annual contributions by its members. The officers' schools provided training during the summer months, when the participants were on vacation from their regular schooling.

The cadets wore beautiful navy uniforms and carried themselves with a pride and dignity enhanced by their habiliments, For the first time, Jewish seamen were being trained to navigate ships and command navy contingents. After the first graduation, the cadets navigated the ship *Sara* from Civitavecchia to Israel. Upon their arrival, they were given a triumphant welcome in the *Beit Ha'am*, the prestigious convention building in Tel Aviv.

When the New Zionist Organization was formed in Vienna, I was already a graduate of the various Betar training courses in Austria and commanded one of Betar's brigades. One day, I was called to report to the commander of the Austrian Betar, Otto Seidman. He asked me whether I would be ready to undertake an extraordinary activity that the high command of Betar wished to entrust to me, namely, the coordination of *Aliyah Bet*, the clandestine immigration to Israel. I asked Seidman why he had chosen *me* for this task. He told me that as a young high school student, an officer of Betar and graduate of its training courses, I was recognized as dedicated and reliable by Betar's leadership. He also thought that, as a student, I would be inconspicuous in the eyes of British agents who were out to obstruct our plans. In the short term, this turned out to be the case, and in the longer run, with unforeseen results.

I agreed—my assurance tempered by trepidation—to take on the responsibility for the organization of the surreptitious migration to Eretz Israel of the Irgun from Austria, Germany, Poland, Romania, Hungary, and Czechoslovakia. We were about to launch our activity with the help of a man who came to Vienna *from* Eretz Israel, Moses Krivoshein, later to be internationally known as Moshe Galili, which I shall call him here. After our introduction by Otto Seidman, I met with Galili in the Hotel Stephanie in Vienna where he resided, and we began to enlist members of Betar ready to join us. My function was to discreetly spread the word within the chapters of the Betar actively functioning in Vienna, that anyone interested in joining our transport register his name. At the time there were some fifteen hundred members in the Austrian

Betar, most of them in Vienna, merely a smattering in the provinces. Soon after our announcement, a small number of youngsters, between seventeen and nineteen years of age, responded. Because of their age, they needed parental approval.

I coordinated my efforts with Mr. Galili. He was the head of this operation, which was named *Af Al Pi Chen* ("despite all)" We were aware of the challenges, but committed to prevail despite all obstacles, and thus chose our name. We were ready to break the British blockade of Eretz Israel, *despite* the British prohibition against a mass Jewish immigration there. Thirty boys were on their way to Greece, where they were to disembark in Piraeus, and leave there on a little boat that we rented in Greece with a Greek captain and crew. Upon its arrival in Haifa, the Irgun amazingly cut the electricity in the harbor and, during the ensuing intentional blackout of about an hour, the passengers left the ship and dispersed.

Though the landing succeeded, we learned from this experience that such an operation would ultimately be impossible on the magnitude we needed. It was inconceivable to bring large numbers of immigrants to the Haifa harbor and cause the equivalent of a short circuit for a longer period of time to enable their disembarking. Far too much risk was involved, that the vessel would be discovered by the British, and the passengers arrested and sent back to their country of origin. This was not, therefore, a practical idea, and so we looked for alternatives. We simply had to find a better location for their landing in Israel, our own D-Day, with as much planning as that assault was later to have.

Eliahu Lankin, a member of the Irgun, along with his friend, Mordecai Paykovich, the older brother of future war hero and Israeli foreign minister Yigal Alon, strode purposefully along the Mediterranean coast, searching for a more convenient beachhead. They finally found it in the Bay of Tantura, near Binyamina between Afula and Hadera in southern Israel.

IN AUGUST 1937, Galili came to Vienna, and we organized a second group of sixty-eight young boys and girls. Shortly thereafter, we organized a third transport of 120 youngsters from Czechoslovakia, Hungary, and Poland. Until their departure for Greece, they were housed in a camp in Kottingbrun, outside of Vienna. Both these transports successfully landed at the new location in Eretz Israel. These were Jewish young people who would otherwise have been forced to remain in a Europe dominated by Hitler. It is not false bravado to claim that their lives were saved as a result of our clandestine operation. That is the word I have always used in describing our operation's mission and accomplishment.

These new immigrants were limited to just one small piece of baggage. They were not permitted to carry passports or identification papers so that, in the event of their capture (always a possibility), they could not be returned to their country of origin, which would be unknown. Their food was provided by the people who worked with Galili in Eretz Israel, Austria, and Greece. Canned food was transported by rail to Greece, where it was brought on board the ships carrying the potential immigrants.

There were no dishes, and there was nothing in the nature of any conveniences. The food was supplied as if the group was going on a Sunday outing, a picnic in the park. It was far from that, almost the diametric opposite, but opponents were everywhere, so any pretext to avoid detection served our purposes.

Unless we were traveling on the wide-open sea, where the passengers could not easily be spotted, they were confined to the cargo section of the boats, which were really nothing more than dilapidated cargo ships. The passengers could at rare times relax on the deck taking a sunbath and watching the sea, but in those stretches when there was any danger of being detected, day or night, they had to be confined to the cargo section, where they had no sleeping areas and only minimal toilet facilities. In later operations, with many more passengers aboard, the problem of accommodation became even more acute. The journey took more than two weeks on the average. Two or three days after a ship and its "cargo" arrived in Greece, the boat was back on the high seas.

After the Nazi takeover of Austria, the necessity of increasing the number of potential immigrants became pressing, a true and immediate matter of life and death. To register new applicants, we utilized an office across the street from the Austrian Ministry of Defense, on the fashionable Stubenring in Vienna. It belonged to the law office of Willi Perl and Bertschi Kornmehl, two leaders of the Revisionist Movement in Austria who became deeply involved in our mission. The news about the clandestine immigration was spreading quickly, and soon many more Austrian Jews came to register.

Among the applicants was a group from Agudath Israel, the orthodox movement to which I once belonged, who were generally opposed to the Zionist idea, but of course not opposed to the idea of self-preservation. Now, some of their members stood trembling in our office when asking for permission to join our transports. They feared our differing ideologies might somehow disqualify them in our eyes. Much to their surprise and relief, I was able to tell them with all sincerity that their opposition to the Zionist idea would not disqualify them from joining our immigration program. Rather, I told them that we were all Jews and the Irgun would welcome them as co-religionists and comrades. They left our office with tears in their eyes and immediately registered to join our transport. Perhaps not entirely fitting my own purist's definition of the Zionist impulse, they were nonetheless now, for all practical purposes, Zionists all, heading to their homeland.

We were in dire need of funds to rent the ships in Greece and cover other expenses. To obtain these funds, Willi Perl, together with the leaders of the Betar in Austria, Otto Seidman and Erich Wolf, met with the notorious Adolf Eichmann at the headquarters of the Gestapo, which he later headed, in the Hotel Metropole in Vienna. Ironically, that five-star, fashionable hotel belonged to a member of the B'rith Hechayal, an affiliate of Betar. The hotel had been requisitioned by the Gestapo when the Nazis occupied the city. Eichmann received our delegation in his office, which had one-way mirrored walls to facilitate surveillance, a security device installed by the Nazis. To make them uneasy, when members of our delegation came into his office, Eichmann put a revolver to their backs and warned them not to converse in Hebrew. In fact, he understood the Hebrew language well from the time when he lived on the outskirts of Tel Aviv, in Saronna, which once belonged to the German Templar Gesellschaft.

The delegation explained their plans to evacuate many Jews in the shortest possible time and bring them to Palestine. They pleaded that the evacuation of Jews was in true conformity with the policy of the Nazi government to make Austria *Judenrein*, free of Jews. At this time the Nazis were not fully convinced of the world's indifference to the plight of the Jews, soon made all too abundantly clear, and the emigration of Jews was more immediately critical to their plans than was extermination. So while it may have almost seemed as if the Jews were in concert with the Nazis, they took no particular comfort in Germany's ostensibly benign intentions, and their motivation for emigration was a combination of Zionism and survival. In terms of their need for foreign currency to rent the ships in Greece, which would carry emigrants away from Germany. Eichmann, although he could have complied in light of his position, did not help. As others have pointed out, he was more a classic German administrator than an ideologue.

Several weeks passed, during which time Perl and his friend Erich Deutsch were imprisoned by the Gestapo in the Rossauerlande barracks in Vienna. When freed, both flew to Berlin to appeal directly to the German ministry of finance for permission to buy English pounds. Before their departure, they met with Erich Rajakovich, a lawyer and at that time superior to Eichmann in the Nazi hierarchy.

Rajakovich, unlike his methodically bureaucratic under-
ling, responded favorably perhaps seeing the "logic"
more clearly than Eichmann, and upon his approval, Perl
and Deutsch received the necessary permit in Berlin to
purchase a small amount of English pound notes, thus
enabling them to secure ships and the necessary provisions. The immigration to Eretz Israel could now expand
and continue to fulfill its mission. The Nazis, incidentally,
would be "rid" of so many Jews.

The Jewish Agency in Palestine, a semi-official but
highly political, British-sanctioned agent of the Jewish
community there, raised many objections to the immigration. Some of its leaders even betrayed our ships to the
British police. Some boats were returned to the ports in
Europe from which they came; others were detained and
their passengers sent to a British detention camp on
Cyprus. British objection to our clandestine immigration
was shared by Jewish leaders such as Abba Hillel Silver.
Such opposition was specifically and obnoxiously
demonstrated by Norman Bentwich, the first attorney
general of Palestine during the period when that country
was occupied by the British army. Bentwich came to
Vienna to systematically oppose the organization of the
immigration, claiming that it would curtail the small
number of certificates that the British allocated to the
Jewish Agency, which in turn went to their political
friends. The collusion being obvious, we intervened with
the authorities in Vienna, and Bentwich was quickly
whisked away from the city.

In August of 1938, a large transport of members of
the Betar from Poland and Lithuania arrived at one of the

train stations in Vienna on their way to Fiume in Italy, where they were to embark on the *Draga I* along with a larger group from Vienna. I waited for them at the northern railway station in Vienna, and while the Nazis were watching me, I supervised the emigrants' transfer to the southern railway station (picture New York City's Penn Station and Grand Central Terminal, then picture getting from one to the other by cab during rush hour) from which they departed to Fiume. The leader of that transport from Eastern Europe was a member of the high command of Betar, Aaron Propes, who later distinguished himself in Israel as the head of the Zimriya, an Israeli choir. Our plan was that their transport would link up in Fiume with my much larger transport from Vienna.

However, while they reached their destination in the transport under my command—originally organized by Willi Perl and Dr. Paul Haller—with 800 passengers on board, the transport was sidetracked by the border police in Arnoldstein, a small Austrian village near Italy's border with Yugoslavia. Our passengers were confined on the train in small compartments, each having room for only six people. Although they were allowed to leave the train during the day, passengers were to return to their compartments at night and had to sleep there in a seated position. During the day, to ease their discomfort and tension, and to assuage the pain in their legs, I organized various sports activities. Keeping their health and morale intact was critical to our purpose. On Friday night and *Shabbat*, prayer services were held in the field outside the train, seeing to their spiritual well-being as well.

An additional impediment to the continuation of our

journey came with the sudden arrival in Arnoldstein of Galili. Perl arrived at around the same time, and he insisted that Galili stay in a nearby hotel. As a ruse to detain him there, Perl removed Galili's clothing "for cleaning," which he returned only when he was leaving Arnoldstein. Perl regarded Galili as a competitor for his leading role in the clandestine immigration, an unusual incidence of personal rivalry in our organization. Due to my association with the *Draga I*, which was a "Perl" ship, my much stronger bond with Galili went unnoticed. After spending two weeks at the railway station in Arnoldstein, since we were not permitted to cross the border into Italy, I decided to leave the transport and go by taxi to the next town, Villach, from where I could call one of the heads of the Gestapo, the same Erich Rajakovich, with whom we had dealt with before. In our telephone conversation, I asked for his intervention with the Italian authorities to allow our transport to proceed over the border. I again importuned him that it was, after all, the policy of the Nazi Party to make Austria as well as Germany *judenrein*. Rajakovich, who was well aware of the policy to speed up the emigration of Jews, promised me he would intervene. To this day I do not know whether he did, but one can imagine him conflicted between the policy and his own unwillingness to deal with Jews in order to accomplish it.

I left Villach that night by cab to return to our transport. When I arrived in Arnoldstein, I was shocked to learn that our train had been ordered to return to Vienna and had, in fact, left the station only minutes before. I asked the taxi driver to bring me back to Villach, the capital of Carinthia, immediately, in the hope I would be able

to catch up with the train. Mid-trip, in the darkness of the
night, the driver offered instead to take me back over the
border to Yugoslavia, which was nearby. He said I could
find safe haven there. I refused this offer, superficially a
sensible, even (perhaps) a gracious one, knowing I was
responsible for the people who had just been ordered to
return to Vienna, and I must catch up with the train. I
begged the driver to speed up so I could catch the train in
Villach.

When we arrived at the railway station at Villach I saw
the lights of the receding train as it pulled away from the
station. I did not even have cash to pay the driver. By sheer
luck, I met the secretary of the Revisionist Party in Vienna
in the restaurant of the railway station, Mr. Bibring.[5] He
lent me the money I needed to pay the driver and to buy a
railway ticket to Vienna. Disappointingly, I was told at the
ticket counter that the next train was a local passenger train
scheduled to arrive in Vienna the following morning. I
bought the ticket and boarded the local and spent a sleep-
less night worrying about the fate of the travelers for whom
I was responsible. Arriving in Vienna at dawn, I found them
lined up with their baggage near the railway tracks, bewil-
dered, despondent, and exhausted, not knowing what their
next move would be. They were afraid they would be taken
to the concentration camp in Dachau, about which word
was spreading, and never be able to continue their journey
to Eretz Israel.

---

[5] How strange it is that this minor chance meeting, which may have
saved my life, was with a man, Mr. Bibring, whose first name I don't
even know or cannot remember. May G-d bless him.

I HAD the displaced passengers reassemble at the Kultursge-meinde, the house where the Jewish Community Council in Vienna was located, a landmark of my childhood. I told them to wait there for further directions. They followed my advice and, with the little money they had, went by taxi to the community house. Meanwhile, I telephoned my superior in Betar, Mordecai Katz, who was back in Fiume waiting for our transport, and reported what had transpired in Arnoldstein. He ordered me to come immediately to Fiume to meet with him. He was determined to organize the continuation of our transport by boat along the Danube to Constantinople, where the passengers would transfer to another vessel that would bring them to Eretz Israel. The complications of these logistics were comparable only to its dangers. Undocumented or questionably documented Jews traveling in Hitler's Europe were subject to persecution, imprisonment, the breakup of families and, ultimately, death.

In compliance with Katz's orders, I went to my parents' home. They were surprised to see me back so soon. I explained to them what had happened and asked my father to give me some money for the purchase of an airline ticket to Italy. I told my parents not to worry, that everything would turn out well. I would speak to them at the first opportunity after I had crossed the border into Italy. I then returned to meet the passengers who were waiting for me at the Jewish Community Council. I informed them, much to their relief but certainly with some apprehension, that they would soon be rerouted by boat on the Danube to Constantinople, from which they would be transferred to yet another vessel that would bring them to Eretz Israel. I then called one of my assistants, who held our passports for safekeeping. He gave me my stateless passport that had an Italian transit visa stamped therein. He also provided me with a fake shipping ticket on an Italian vessel, the *Socrates* (see page 215), that Perl had rented and paid for. Perl later learned that he had been taken in by a group of swindlers. The vessel never existed.

When I arrived at the Viennese airport in Aspang to board the plane to Venice, I was detained by an SS officer, who ushered me into a small interrogation room. He said he knew that I had spent last night in Arnoldstein and searched me for money. It was against the law to have in one's possession more than ten Reichsmarks. This was the maximum of German currency that Jews were permitted to take out of Austria. I proved to the officer that I did not violate this restriction and he would not find more than ten marks in my possession. During my detention, I became impatient, fearful of missing my plane, but I did not want to alert the officer to my nervousness. I told him, in my clear Viennese dialect, that he would be accountable to his superiors for holding up the emigration of Jews from Austria if he detained me much longer. Frightened, he relented and allowed me to race to the plane. Five traveling companions (four young men and one girl, members of the Betar in Germany) whom I had asked to accompany me to Fiume, were already in their seats after passing a lesser interrogation. While they all had passports from their German or Austrian countries of origin, my statelessness had delayed me, and quite possibly exposed me to some additional risk. When I climbed the steps to the biplane, the propellers were already running. I winked to my colleagues signaling them not to speak to me or even acknowledge me during the flight. We were soon flying over the snow-covered Alps to Venice where we boarded a passenger train to Fiume.

IN THE middle of the flight, I remembered that my ship ticket for the *Socrates* was not filled in properly. I quickly inserted my name, shaking while writing, in part due to the plane's erratic movement, in part due to the condition of my nerves.

In Venice, my colleagues and I were met by the Italian customs officer. He inspected our passports which had an Italian transit visa stamped in it. We "explained," dissembling, that we were students on our way to Fiume, where we would join a cruise on the Mediterranean. We were admitted to Venice. I immediately telephoned my aunt in Vienna. My parents had no phone at their home, and I gave her the good news that I was safely over the border. I noticed many joyous people bustling around the amazing streets of Venice, such as the Rialto, as seemed to be their daily custom of an evening. We boarded a luxurious Italian train, and, on the way to Fiume, I saw through my window a large concentration of soldiers bivouacking on Italy's border with Yugoslavia. We made a short stop in Trieste, where the station was decorated with German and Italian flags to welcome a forthcoming visit by Benito Mussolini, Italy's fascist dictator. I went to the restaurant to buy a cup of coffee. A Romanian Jew standing near the counter asked me where I was heading. When I told him that I was going to Palestine, he warned me that I would do better to go with him to Romania, as Palestine was in turmoil because of the Arab riots. In response, I suggested that he ought to leave Romania as soon as it was possible as *he* was the one in jeopardy.

When I arrived in Fiume, Italy,[6] I reported immediately to Mordecai Katz, who eagerly expected me to assume command of the *Draga I,* which was just about to arrive from Greece. I had come to Fiume penniless. One of my friends on the transport solicited Jewish businessmen in town to lend us Italian currency so that we would have pocket money with us during our brief stay. He explained our situation as refugees from Austria traveling to Eretz Israel on the clandestine boat. The Jewish businessmen he approached generously responded to his appeal, and we received enough Italian currency to spend judiciously during our transient stay. It was even adequate to allow us a short visit by bus to the Italian resort of Volosca, where we spent a much-needed evening relaxing from the trials and tribulations of the recent weeks, and in preparation for the ensuing ones.

Upon our return to Fiume, Katz ordered us to be ready for embarkation on the *Draga I* by midnight. On our way to the boat, we were accompanied by friendly Italian *carabinieri,* who assisted us in boarding. On the boat, I met the representative of the Irgun Tzv'ai Leumi, Shmuel Dagansky (Johnny). We shared responsibility for the transport. While I was responsible for the European

---

6 Fiume is the port-city's Italian name. Across the bay, the Yugoslavian part was known as Reikavik. Today, it is a Croatian city called Rijeka.

contingent of passengers, Johnny would be in charge of the landing arrangements in Eretz Israel. Three miles outside the territorial waters of Italy, we spotted a little row boat with three passengers who came from Yugoslavia to join us in the middle of the sea as they had not been permitted to cross a little bridge in Fiume that linked the countries. When we picked them up, I was astonished that they did not bring any luggage with them other than a guitar.

Oh, but wasn't that guitar a blessing! We continued to sail happily along the coastline of the Adriatic Sea, singing Betar's songs to the stringed accompaniment of the very talented musician. To avoid being spotted by British intelligence, the passengers were required to stay below deck most of the time. One of the Greek officers graciously allowed me to use his cabin.

On the upper deck, next to the captain, stood Victor Bleicher, a member of the Viennese Betar and a graduate of our maritime school in Civitavecchia, watching the compass as we intended. When we crossed the Canal of Corinth, all passengers were required to remain below, as it was dangerous to be spotted from hills on either side of the narrow channel. We reached Piraeus, outside of Athens, where we docked in the bay. It was *Erev* (the evening preceding) Rosh Hashanah.

Unexpectedly and extortionately, the crew demanded from us that we secure from our Israeli comrades a larger remuneration for their services, and they threatened to "strike" until they received the increase. We were stranded in the Bay of Piraeus for three days. By Morse Code we were able to communicate with the Irgun in Eretz Israel requesting that the captain's demand be met; we were, in effect, trapped. Our only hope might have been seizing the controls. We had a naval crew acting as passengers, but the risks involved in such a move might have jeopardized the future of the entire immigration scheme.

On Rosh Hashanah I placed two little candles on the prow of the ship and asked the passengers to attend a religious service in celebration of the High Holiday. I volunteered to be the cantor and led the service, a memorable one because of the circumstances. During our prayers, we could see Athens illuminated at night, far away from our landing place. I thought how fortunate were those people who did not have to share our destiny as Jews, to be constantly hounded and persecuted. Within three days, the Greek captain of *Draga I* was informed by his superiors that the money he had asked for had been deposited in their account. Our peril-fraught journey could now continue.

Leaving Piraeus, we entered the very stormy Ionian Sea where we transferred to a smaller boat that would bring us to the shores of Eretz Israel. Thoughts of Homer crossed my mind as we sailed the Hellenic waters; our trip had certainly been something of an odyssey, with dangers, it seemed, at every juncture. Hanging onto the mooring which linked the vessels together we managed to board the smaller boat, which would bring us to our destination. The only "difficulty" we experienced was in helping a pregnant woman hanging on to the rope while she was trying to reach the smaller boat, which was easily accomplished.

We arrived at the territorial waters of Eretz Israel in three days. Sailing parallel to the seashore, we saw the magnificent sunset and Haifa's beautiful Mount Carmel. We sailed from Atlit in the south to the north near Haifa.

Standing on the deck at night, Johnny, my colleague from the Irgun, and I anxiously awaited the special signal that would permit us to land. Our food supply had been depleted, and there was a severe shortage of water. We ate only bagels—stale biscuits—that had to be moistened by seawater to be eaten, which only exacerbated our thirst.

Meanwhile, Yom Kippur had started. We fasted as Jews are biblically commanded to do on the Day of Atonement. Several hours elapsed, and we still saw no signal. Outside the three-mile zone, we recited the Kol Nidre, the stirring prayer specific to that night, with great emotion. In his book, *Years of Wrath, Days of Glory: Memoirs from the Irgun,* Yitshaq Ben-Ami writes: "Our first voyage, independent of Galili, was the *Draga I.* It sailed from Fiume, Italy, under the command of Max Stock [yours truly, the author], piloted by Shmuel Tagansky of the Irgun. It landed in Tantura on Yom Kippur eve (October 19, 1938) after an emotional Kol Nidre service on deck. . . ." Yom Kippur night in Israel is always illuminated by a full moon. The Jewish calendar is lunar. This posed a great danger for us in landing without being observed by the British navy. At about ten o'clock that night, while holding on to the rail of the boat, I spotted the long-awaited signal from the harbor in the bay of Tantura. We slowly proceeded to approach the shore. The passengers beneath the deck were terribly frightened, not realizing they were about to land, but feeling only the rocking and the noise of the waves beating against the boat. Soon, we spotted three little rowboats approaching us. We were so close to land at that point that we allowed anyone who was able to swim across to do so. The remaining passengers were taken ashore in rowboats by members of the Irgun, each of whom carried a rifle across his shoulder. They greeted us with a hearty welcome of Shalom! and they assured us that we should not be afraid; they would help us to land safely. Some of the passengers jumped into the sea and swam to the beach. Others, including myself, landed on shore by boat. By moonlight we could clearly see some passengers on land throwing themselves to the ground to kiss the holy earth of Eretz Israel. Soldiers of the Irgun stood in formation along the landing area. They accompanied us over a two-mile stretch of sand dunes to the nearest police station, in Benyamina, where we were ordered to stay over for the holy day Yom Kippur until our dispersal the following day. The boat that had brought us to Eretz Israel meanwhile returned to Greece while we were on our way to Benyamina. The Arabs were rioting at the time, and every police station was equipped with a spotlight on its watchtower to illuminate the adjacent orange groves, searching for Arab marauders. To deflect attention from the immigrants, the spotlights were positioned that night to omit the illumination of a triangle leading from the coastline to the police station. That night, members of the Irgun had invited the British police constables stationed in Benyamina to a drinking party in the nearby town of Hadera. The Irgun members closely but covertly watched to ensure that the British constables did not return to their posts before our transport had dispersed early the following morning.

The morning after, buses manned by members of the Irgun arrived, to distribute us, the "illegal" but delighted immigrants, to various destinations in the country. Some went to the settlements of Betar. Others, including myself, chose to go to Tel Aviv. Passing through Hadera, I noticed the surprisingly verdant agricultural development while inhaling the fragrant scent of the orange groves. In Tel Aviv, I met my grandmother, uncles and aunts, who had each arrived on a capitalist immigration certificate (an assurance of solvency) that my Uncle Aaron had sent them. They came by way of Trieste, traveling on the Italian luxury liner *Galileo* and arriving one day before my own, less luxurious appearance. They were surprised to see me arrive so soon after they had. I came, of course, without the British sanction I had spurned, but my parents, playing by the rules, had still not been able to make the voyage by legal means.

As soon as I came to Tel Aviv, in October 1938, I urged my uncle at the Anglo-Palestine Bank to send new certificates of immigration to my parents immediately, conscious of the extraordinarily dangerous situation in Austria after the invasion of Nazi Germany. Through his offices, the certificates had already been sent to the Jewish Agency for them, not once but twice. However, the Agency's office in Vienna gave them away to other applicants, precedence appallingly being given, as we have seen, to political supporters of the Agency. My parents' departure from a growingly threatening Austria, where conditions were only worsening, had been twice postponed.

Frightened for them, I made the dangerous journey from Tel Aviv to Jerusalem, a particularly hazardous overland trip because of the Arab unrest that exploded in 1938 and 1939. This violent and fearful insurgency was aimed at Jews whose continuing influx threatened Arab plans to control the territory. In Jerusalem, I asked the assistance of my cousin, Esther Pann,[7] the wife of the founder of the Bezalel School of Art, the famous Israeli painter Abel Pann. She took me to meet an acquaintance, the head of the Jewish Agency's Immigration Division, Chaim Barlas, whom we hoped might be able to expedite the granting of entry visas for my parents. By this two-pronged strategy we hoped to encourage both Aaron Vardi, my uncle at the bank, and the Jewish Agency itself, to do the proper thing by granting my parents entry.

On the way to Barlas' office, Cousin Esther pointed out a man who was walking along the street at that moment, identifying him as the son of the First High Commissioner of Palestine, Sir Herbert Samuel. This pedestrian was himself the commissioner of immigration of the government of Palestine, Mr. Edwin Samuel. I facetiously suggested to Esther that we should move to the other side of the street as I was not a "legal" immigrant. Years later, history working in its peculiar ways, I became his assistant and close confidante, and we acted as co-founders of the Jerusalem Tutorial Classes.

We were assured by Mr. Barlas that the visa for my parents would be issued by the British Consulate in Vienna immediately, and that they would follow through this time and get it in the proper hands, and I was greatly relieved.

---

[7] Esther's father Eldad, and my father, were brothers, but I never met him. Unfortunately, Eldad passed away in Poland at a young age. Esther named one of her sons after him but he, too, sadly, yet nobly, met an untimely end. He was killed in the line of duty, in the defense of his people and his country. The Arabs who captured and killed him, gruesomely returned his remains in severed pieces in a bag.

Mordecai at 4 years old.

Portrait at 10 years old.

BELOW: Outing with Mordecai's elementary school, standing fifth from right.

LEFT: Ze'ev Vladimir Jabotinsky, fighter for Jewish sovereignty in Israel, Commander of the Jewish Brigade in the British army in World War I.
CENTER: Theodor Herzl, visionary of Jewish statehood.
RIGHT: Passport picture issued to Mordecai by the Nazis before he left Vienna.

Betar, an organization which emulated the Maccabees, who rose 2000 years ago against the Hellenistic Conquerors that tried to extinguish the Jewish spirit. The Maccabees were few and poorly armed, and fought against the mighty forces of the Greeks. However, they were valiant, fierce, and unyielding and they won! They restored religious freedom and nationhood to their people. Betar had a similar vision of rebuilding the ancient homeland of the Jews. In this picture, Betarim marching in parade, Mordecai is the drummer on the left.

Betar's leader and commander-in-chief Ze'ev Vladimir Jabotinsky reviewing the cadets, surrounded by commanders, including Arye Korpert, Seidman and Goldstein.

Mordecai and his parents going to a family wedding in Jerusalem.

ABOVE LEFT: Mordecai and Viscount Edwin Samuels, his friend and mentor for over fifty years.
ABOVE RIGHT: Abba Eben, Mordecai's long time friend, teacher, and colleague.

ABOVE: David Ben Gurion attending an office party at Mordecai's office in the Kirya.
RIGHT: Israel's Foreign Minister and Mordecai's boss, Moshe Sharet, with Mordecai (right).

Leonard Bernstein performed for Israeli troops after the state was declared and received a hero's welcome for his courageous support. Present at the reception in his honor are James McDonald, the first U.S. Amabassador, Mordecai Hacohen, Golda Meir, and Naomi Granot, daughter of the president of the Jewish National Fund.

ABOVE LEFT: Prime Minister Yitzhak Rabin and Mordecai had been in the Israeli delegation to Rhodes for the Armistice negotiations with Egypt after the war of Independence.

ABOVE RIGHT: Deputy Prime Minister Shimon Peres receiving Mordecai in his office.

LEFT: Ariel Sharon espoused brave, bold ideas about a strong and safe land of Israel within its historic borders.

Mordecai presenting his father's book to Israel's third president, Zalman Shazar.

Mordecai with Dr. Israel Eldad, author, teacher, and Ideological Leader of the Lechi.

BELOW LEFT: Yaakov Meridor was Mordecai's commander in the Irgun Zevai Leumi, a pre-Statehood underground movement.

BELOW RIGHT: Mordecai with Itzhak Ben Ami, who had played a major part in the clandestine immigration.

Mordecai represented Israel at the United Nations Inaugural Conference on Public Personnel Management.

OPPOSITE TOP: Saul Kagan joins Mordecai Aviezer and Mordecai reminiscing about the days in 1948 leading up to the siege of Jerusalem.

OPPOSITE BOTTOM: Mordecai (seventh from the right) representing Israel at the United Nations conference with members of the conference and Secretary General of the UN Trygve Lie.

ABOVE LEFT: Sir Isaac Wolfson at a reception in Jerusalem, meeting some of Mordecai's old friends, the journalist Moshe Meisels, and the internationally renowned violinist Zvi Zeitlin.

ABOVE RIGHT: Yom Haatzmaut in Geneva at which Swiss Senator Fisse and Mordecai were the featured speakers.

The welcome awaiting Mordecai by the Jewish community in Teheran, Iran, where he helped build Ozar Hatorah schools. The Hebrew text of the sign reads "Welcome Dr. Mordecai Hacohen."

Before my parents arrived in Tel Aviv, the only request my father made was that he stay in a rented apartment not wanting to impose upon me. And so, upon their eventual arrival, we all went directly from the harbor in Haifa to a leased apartment in a fashionable district of Tel Aviv, about eighty miles south, on Ben Yehuda Street near the corner of Gordon Street. Some of my extended family lived across the street. A few days later, my parents' luggage arrived. Though my father was once in the shipping business, he did not send or bring a whole crate of personal belongings, as he could have easily afforded. He brought only the very minimum that he could safely ship out of Austria, which included a few valuable or sentimental possessions, such my mother's silver candlesticks, my golden bar mitzvah watch chain, Persian rugs, and precious family memorabilia.

WITH MY parents now living safely in Tel Aviv, my direct involvement in the clandestine immigration ended, and I enrolled at the Hebrew University in Jerusalem. I rented a room which I shared with an old friend of mine from Vienna, who later became the attorney general of Israel, Erwin Schayowitz Shimron, in a boarding house across the street from the Jewish Agency. Shimron, too, had been a member of Betar in Vienna, and was now a student in the faculty of law at the Hebrew University. To support himself, he joined the Israeli auxiliary police as a "*gafir*," an auxiliary policeman during these times of the Arab riots.

The salary of a *gafir*, six English pounds, was sufficient to maintain an entire family. But Erwin's job was enormously hazardous. Every day, when my roommate had to go to the Old City on police duty, Jews were being murdered by Arabs. When I came home each evening, I opened the door apprehensively, with a prayer on my lips that I would find my roommate alive.

During the week, I would frequently stay with my parents in an apartment that they had rented on Hayarkon Street in Tel Aviv after the short period on Ben Yehuda Street. It was small, but had a magnificent view of the Mediterranean. We spent our first holiday together. On Sukkot, I built a *sukkah* on the roof of that building, and decorated it with the Persian rugs that my parents had sent from Vienna.

One night we were suddenly awakened by signals that sounded like an SOS. This was usually a frightening noise, accompanying some tragic incident. I looked out the window, and this time saw many people, some of them still in their nightwear, running to the shore. The rumor spread amongst the crowd via shouting that a boat with "illegal" immigrants had arrived. Indeed, this was true. As I recall, this was the "*Parita.*" I joined the masses in the street, running to see the new immigrants. When I got there, I found that the British police had cordoned off the area. The boat had been navigated in such a way that it was now stuck in the sand and could not be moved. I stayed together with many other residents of the area for the rest of the night.

In the morning, the British army and police brought buses to move the passengers to a military camp in Sarafand between Tel Aviv and Jerusalem. Standing on the corner of Hayarkon and Trumpledor Street, I watched the buses passing by. I suddenly heard a loud voice emanating from one of the buses. An immigrant had recognized his father standing on the sidewalk observing the British police removing the refugees. When he luckily spotted his father through the window of the bus, he cried out to him in Yiddish, *"Tate, ich bin do! "*— ("Father, I am here!") to announce that he had arrived safely. This episode will always remain in my memory as a symbol of the clandestine immigration I had helped to organize. More and more of us were "here" all the time, and here was certainly better than there.

Another ship, the *Sakarya*, had more than a thousand passengers aboard when it arrived in Haifa harbor, and was unofficially led by Ze'ev Jabotinsky's son, Eri Jabotinsky. The boat had been captured and Eri Jabotinsky interrogated. He was charged with bringing Jews illegally to Palestine. He told the British that he was a citizen of Eretz Israel who was accompanied to Haifa by one thousand of his close friends. Some of the passengers, who tried to save themselves jumped from the boat and drowned in the harbor. Eri Jabotinsky was sent to Acco Prison where his father had been incarcerated years earlier.

Eri was sentenced to serve until the end of the war. Ze'ev Jabotinsky died while on a visit to a Betar summer camp in Hunter, New York. The year was 1940. When he died, they found only small change in his pocket, the total extent of his worldly possessions. His son was temporarily released from prison upon his father's death and was able to join us at a mass memorial rally in the stadium of Tel Aviv.

The Irgun brought many ships to Eretz Israel, most with successful landings. There was one tragic exception which I witnessed, the arrival of the *"Tiger Hill"*, which was attacked and captured by the British navy within sight of the shore. With military precision, they shot several passengers at sea, whom they considered to be criminals. An atrocity in itself, this mass murder underscored the risky nature of our immigration program. I was standing with many colleagues in the Irgun, in the water outside the beach of Tel Aviv, fighting the waves, singing "Hatikvah" and the anthem of the Irgun as the bodies of the executed passengers were loaded onto navy boats.

Although I have been stressing the role of Betar in the organization of many ships in the clandestine immigration, I must repeat, in fairness to complete historic truth, the involvement of the Haganah, the indigenous Israeli forces, with whom we not always agreed. The most famous among them, the *"Exodus,"* was made famous by Leon Uris in his eponymous novel, later made into an Otto Preminger masterpiece. I am fully conscious of the efforts made by the brave men and women of the Haganah, occasional rivals, who risked their lives to save many Jews from Europe.

There is a monument on the beach at Tel Aviv, shaped like waves, commemorating the campaign and listing the ships involved. When the time comes to remember the organizers, the people, of the clandestine immigration, I recommend a fitting memorial at some appropriate location. They deserve lasting recognition.

תל חי

Life in Israel

"Putting Feathers on the Israelis"

After what turned out to be a transitory sojourn in Tel Aviv, my parents settled in Jerusalem, the city which typified the Eretz Israel that my father always sought. At that time my father insisted he wanted the family to live together. My parents and I then rented an apartment in a modern house in Jerusalem, the Beit Ha Maalot. It was close to the Jewish Agency on King George Avenue, across the street from the famous Bezalel Museum. The building was made of the unique and beautiful "Jerusalem Stone," and had an elevator straight to our apartment, an unusual luxury in that part of the world at the time. We enjoyed all the conveniences that a modern house could offer, and from our large balcony we had a magnificent view of the mountains of Judea.

On our first *Shabbat* in Jerusalem, my father and I went to the Western Wall. In the narrow alley fronting that wall, my father indicated a man standing there, covered only by half of his prayer shawl while the other half was almost falling off his shoulder. When the two saw each other, they began to circle around until my father called out his name "Chachkes!" The man responded, "Srul!" This man, Chachkes, was pseudonymously the great author S. Y. Agnon who, like my father, had been born in Buzcacz, grew up in the synagogue of the Rabbi of Czor—ov, and where they studied modern Hebrew together. Interestingly, I later came to know Simon Wiesenthal, the legendary Nazi-hunter, who hailed from the same small town. Wiesenthal devoted his life to tracking down German war criminals who had fled after committing unspeakable atrocities. One of thousands of war criminals Wiesenthal exposed was Adolf Eichmann, who was ultimately captured in Argentina.

Agnon, like my father, had always been an ardent Zionist and belonged to Hovevei Zion, a forerunner of the Zionist movement. After this friendly encounter at the Western Wall, my parents and I were invited to Agnon's home in Talpiot outside of Jerusalem for a leisurely evening of reminiscences.

When my father passed away, I wrote a composition describing his personality to be inscribed on his tombstone. By using the letters of his name, I created an acrostic recapitulating his virtues. Before having it cut into the masonry, I read what amounted to my poem in Hebrew to Agnon, who approved it. When my mother passed away in New York later and was brought by me for interment next to my father on Har haMenuchot in Jerusalem, I had her tombstone chiseled to form another Hebrew acrostic of mine. I was gratified that Agnon, to whom I read it, again gave his agreement that it would be fitting. As the expression has it, the words were etched in stone.

On Agnon's visit to New York years later, I was privileged to meet with him and present him with a copy of my father's book, *Kitzur Toldat Chochmei Yisroel*, a biography of the early sages of ancient Israel, *Tannaim* and *Amoraim*. Agnon posed with my sons and myself for a photograph on this occasion. For his outstanding literary achievements, Agnon became the first Israeli to be awarded the Nobel Prize for Literature, presented to him by the King of Norway in 1966.

I searched for work to support my aging parents and myself. A friend of my father in Paris, Maurice Schlitner, who had once worked in our family's business in Vienna, was a manufacturer of artificial feathers and flowers for the fashion industry. Knowing that we had arrived with only limited means, he wrote to suggest that we sell his merchandise in Israel, and soon thereafter sent a supply of samples. Ladies do not normally wear hats, with or without feathers, in Israel, because of the hot climate. Who could envision that there would be an interest in artificial flowers and feathers for decorations on their non-existent hats, dresses, or on anything else?

But I accepted the offer and went from store to store in Jerusalem to find fashion outlets showing an interest in our merchandise, or creating one. Selling ice to Eskimos. I succeeded in selling the artificial flowers and feathers, having considerably marked up the price to yield a good profit. In no time the first consignment was sold, and I soon received a larger one. My business expanded to Tel Aviv and Haifa from Jerusalem, and it gradually developed into a profitable enterprise in all three cities. My mother used to laugh at me, "Mordecai, you are putting feathers on the Israelis!"

One shipment after another arrived and profitably sold. The last shipment in 1942 remained inaccessible in a warehouse at the harbor of Marseilles. The Germans, who invaded France, confiscated all the goods in the warehouses. Once again I found myself without any income to support my studies and my parents. I then tried my luck in the textile business, having now acquired some skill in salesmanship. I met a refugee from Poland, a textile importer, who maintained a small store in Jerusalem. Despite the fact that the price of textiles was constantly rising as a result of the war, the limitation of shipping space, and the lack of hard currency, all the while increasing our profits, after a while I left that business. It did not allow me ample time to be a full-time student.

At the Hebrew University, I had little choice but to enroll in courses such as history, philosophy, and Hebrew literature, which were not my true preferences. My teachers included renowned authorities on the subjects they taught: Professor Yitzhak Baer taught Jewish history in the Middle Ages, and was an expert on the history of the Jews in Spain; Professor Yellin taught us Hebrew; and Professor Leon Roth— brother of historian Cecil Roth—lectured on modern philosophy. I was fortunate to take courses with the distinguished philosopher Professor Martin Buber. But my most beloved and respected teacher was Professor Josef Klausner, who, like Buber (and my father), had been to the First Zionist Congress in Basel in 1897. He lectured on the history of modern Hebrew literature.

Although Klausner was an expert in the history of the Second Temple, he was not allowed to teach that subject because the president of the University, Yehuda Magnes,

and other members of the B'rith Shalom advocated a bi-
national state for Arabs and Jews, and therefore thought
Klausner's beliefs on the subject might be too "nationalis-
tic," an example of both Israeli and academic political
infighting. During the riots of the late 1930s, as I stated
earlier, it was quite dangerous to travel by bus to the university on Mount Scopus, which I needed to do every day.
The bus ascended through winding roads with its windows protected by steel bars. Passing through Arab
neighborhoods, the passengers were frequently shot at by
the residents. On one of its last journeys to the university,
before the War of Independence, a bus was attacked by a
mob of Arabs who killed all of its passengers including
many prominent professors. Among those victims was
the fiancé of the daughter of Israel's prime minister David
Ben-Gurion. It was devastating to see her in mourning. It
took a long time for her to recover from the shock of los-
ing her boyfriend, an immigrant from Romania, who was
also her colleague in the science faculty of the university.
Despite the tragedy, she completed her studies and was
awarded a doctorate.

During Israel's War of Independence a decade later,
access to the Hebrew University became literally impossible when the route passing near Arab houses in Sheik
Sharah became even more intolerably dangerous. The
Arabs were fearful that, if the Jews would blow the
Shofar at the Western Wall in Jerusalem, they might summon the Messiah, who would supplant their Allah. Thus,
the Arabs started to riot as early as 1929, when the Jews
blew the Shofar, as is traditional on the High Holidays. As
a result of the outbursts that year, the British Mandatory

Administration prohibited the blowing of the Shofar at the Western Wall. Every subsequent year on Rosh Hashanah or Yom Kippur when someone blew the Shofar, he was arrested by the British secret police and sentenced, usually to six months in prison in the old city.

On Rosh Hashanah and Yom Kippur the Jewish congregations necessarily had to move to the massive Great Synagogue, the Churba Synagogue, to listen to the blowing of the Shofar. Incidentally, during the War of Liberation ten years later, the Arabs destroyed that famous synagogue once known for its medieval rabbi Yehuda Hachassid. It has only recently been reconstructed in a masterwork of architectural restoration.

Despite being a secular group, the Irgun Tzv'ai Leumi organized a group, which they called *Plugat Hatokin.* The group was essentially a brigade of Shofar-blowers who sounded their horns at the conclusion of Yom Kippur services, in calculatedly open defiance to the British. I vividly remember the last Yom Kippur (1947) that I prayed at the Western Wall, shortly before sunset as was religiously commanded. The British secret police, CID, lined up in the narrow lane across from the Western Wall. But this time, the IZL outsmarted them. At the end of the service a boy at one end of the Western Wall simulated a Shofar sound by blowing into his clenched hand. Immediately, the secret police ran to catch the child. While they ran after him, a boy on the other end of the Western Wall blew a real Shofar. The police immediately turned around to catch that fellow, but we all started singing "Hatikvah," the national anthem. There was a protocol that when the Israeli National Anthem is being sung, the police cannot move and must stay in place. During this lull, the boy who blew the Shofar disappeared and escaped capture. We rejoiced and danced all the way from the Western Wall to Jaffa Road singing the songs of the Betarim.

I became active in the Students' Organization of the Hebrew University and was elected to the Executive Committee of the *Yabneh VeYodephet* Fraternity, affiliated with the Jabotinsky Movement. The president of our Students' Organization was Dr. Aron Kachalsky, a brother of professor Ephraim Katzir, who later became the president of Israel. A renowned scientist, Dr. Aron Kachalsky was killed years later in an assault at the Lod Airport carried out by a Japanese terrorist. Another prominent president of the Students' Organization was Gideon Hausner, who later, as attorney general of Israel, was the prosecutor at the trial of the notorious Nazi war criminal Adolf Eichmann. Other classmates included Rabbi Shlomo Goren, who went on to become the chief chaplain of the Israeli army and eventually the Chief Rabbi of Israel. He was one of the first soldiers to reach the Western Wall when Jerusalem was liberated during the Six Day War in 1967.

Finances continued to be a worrisome problem. To maintain my studies and help my parents, I had to find a job that would secure a minimum livable income and allow me to study at the university. I even considered the possibility of joining the service of the British Mandatory Government, but being an "illegal" immigrant, this proved very difficult. I always enjoyed classical music, and attended the weekly concerts of the Palestine

Broadcasting Orchestra. I befriended a famous violinist who at present is Professor of Music at the Eastman School of the University of Rochester in New York State. A native of Israel of Russian parentage, Zvi Zeitlin studied in America. He often appeared in recitals and as a soloist with the orchestra. At one of these concerts, we met the daughter of the Chief Clerk of the British War Supply Board in Palestine, Aliza Sperling, of blessed memory. She later intervened on my behalf with her father, and soon after I was offered a job with the Controller of Light Industries, a branch of the British War Supply Board. During the war, the government imposed many restrictions on the importation of various merchandise, which required shipping space or hard currency. Controls were instituted on commodities related to light industry, heavy industry, and even food.

The chief clerk hired me without asking any questions about my resident status, nor about my background, and certainly not about my involvement with Betar, which was out of favor with the new Israeli power structure. He assigned me to the Statistics Department of the Controller of Light Industries, and I was very sorry to learn later that he was tragically killed in the explosion at the King David Hotel, the target of an attack by the Irgun Tzv'ai Leumi, where he had served at the headquarters of the government of Palestine. Before the explosion, the chief secretary of the government ignored repeated warnings by the Irgun and did not permit the staff to leave the building in time. The Statistics department was located in a beautiful modern building near the Anglo-Palestine Bank and the Central Post Office on Jaffa Road in Jerusalem. I had to deal with records and monthly reports on textile goods and yarn supplies. These reports came in from manufacturers and importers. My salary, fifteen pounds per month, included fringe benefits and provisions for vacations. As an observant Jew, I was not required to work on Shabbat or Jewish holidays. My monthly salary was more than double what other civil servants earned, and double the monthly living expenses of an entire family.

During this time, my father, advancing in age, took on a part-time job as an accountant. He did not know English, but his command of Hebrew was excellent, and he had no problem communicating on the job. My mother started a business of her own, and developed a fine clientele in Jerusalem to whom she sold textile piece goods.

I rapidly advanced in my own position. The Statistics department constantly grew and added additional employees, among them German refugees who held Ph.D. degrees from European universities. The head of my department, Mr. Gillon, studied in England, and married the daughter of a British admiral after her conversion to Judaism. He appreciated my work and named me his assistant. I was ultimately promoted to the rank of Inspector, and my income grew accordingly.

Due to the climatic conditions in the country, we started working at 7:30 in the morning and were free to go home by 2:30 in the afternoon. This convenient schedule afforded me ample time to attend courses at the university and also to play tennis in the afternoon in Rechavia, a beautiful district in Jerusalem.

Later, our offices moved to new quarters at the Terra Sancta Building on Mamilla Road. Before the government rented it for its various departments of the War Supply Board the house had been a convent, thus the Latinate name. In addition to my duties, which involved the tabulation of statistical reports, my colleagues and I were given the responsibility of granting licenses for the importation of textile machinery. The textile industry in Eretz Israel had just begun to develop although the British government administration in Palestine was certainly not interested in assisting in its development. Rather, it had always been fearful of encouraging a competition with the textile industry in England. They thought it would hurt the export of English textiles if they permitted the growth of a local textile industry in their protectorate. It was a time-tested historical conflict, rooted in colonialism, which had contributed nearly two centuries before to the American Revolution. The British high priority this time was to support the war effort against Nazi Germany, and, therefore it was imperative for them to allow the establishment of a textile industry in Israel despite their more general reservations.

In the course of time, my duties expanded further, and I was given the responsibility to issue import licenses for precious gems. The diamond industry had just begun to develop, thanks to the immigration of Romanian and Belgian Jews. The immigrants from Romania had considerable financial resources at their disposal, which they wisely invested in the diamond industry. It made them wealthy within a short period of time. The immigrants from Belgium brought with them an expertise in the diamond industry, having been prominent diamond merchants in Europe. The importation and production of industrial diamonds was given priority due to their importance to the war effort.

I must say that I was initially very disappointed that my original ambition to study at the school for diplomats in Geneva was rendered impossible when World War II broke out and I had to abandon my youthful aspirations. The Hebrew University did not provide training facilities in applicable diplomatic disciplines. Since my teenage years I had dreamed of serving the government of the Jewish state I had hoped would emerge in my lifetime. A state means not only a flag or the display of other national symbols, it also means good government administration, a postman who can deliver the mail, a sanitation department that can keep the streets clean, a police force, and an army that is trained to defend its citizens.

No training facilities for civil service positions existed in Israel at the time. The Zionist leaders believed that they could train the civil service after the State of Israel had come into existence, a recurrence of their lack of vision and foresight regarding the building of a navy.

The man who had once been pointed out to me while strolling down a street, Edwin Samuel, the son of the first High Commissioner of Palestine, Sir Herbert Samuel, in a series of lectures at the YMCA in Jerusalem, announced that he planned to organize tutorial classes for the training of students in public administration. This was in keeping with my Jabotinskian vision of Jewish progress, and I became intensely interested. Indeed, it was something I had come to believe in strongly, but by the time I made up my mind to enroll in his courses, the time limit for registration had expired. I called on Samuel at his office where he served as the Imperial Censor for the Middle East. Postal censorship was important during the war to protect the country against espionage and subversion. It also became necessary to control the outflow of hard currency and prevent illegal financial transactions. Samuel turned me down, saying that the registration deadline had passed, but soon changed his mind. He made an exception, and agreed to admit me, adding that he admired my persistence. I took the opportunity to invite him to listen to a program that I was about to broadcast in observance of the seventh anniversary of the annexation of Austria by Nazi Germany. To prepare my half-hour radio program, I had worked for several weeks to record the history of Viennese Jewry, describing its great contributions to European and world culture.

The broadcast was well received by the public and the press. A week later, Edwin Samuel invited me for tea. Samuel's house in the Talbiya quarter of Jerusalem was a beautiful mansion that belonged to an Armenian resident and was named after him, the Matossian House. It was located in a very exclusive residential section of Jerusalem overlooking the district of Katamon, occupied mainly by wealthy Arabs. The neighborhood had a mixed population of Jews and Arabs, many of them senior government officers or prosperous merchants. Samuel congratulated me on the radio program, which he listened to with great interest. He revealed to me that he had been eager to hear the broadcast because he was slated to become the next director of the Palestine Broadcasting System, PBS, a separate government department for broadcasting that was just being organized independent of the Post Office

Administration with which Samuel, as the Imperial Censor, was affiliated.

Having initially turned me down as an applicant, Samuel now asked my assistance in the organization of the proposed Jerusalem Tutorial Classes. He planned this institution with the hope that it would ultimately become a college of public administration. No such school existed in the Middle East. I was flattered by his offer, but I declined. I did not think I was qualified to hold that position and, in good conscience, could not accept it.

Astonished, Samuel asked for my reasons. I said I felt that my command of the English language was not proficient enough to work with a personality of his stature. Secondly, as a government officer I was not permitted to accept any other job without permission from the head of my department. In addition, as an observant Jew I would not be able to work on Shabbat or Jewish holidays; finally, I said, I was a Zionist who strongly believed in the establishment of a Jewish state in our time. I purposely mentioned this because I was aware that Sir Herbert Samuel, his father, when he was high commissioner of Palestine, unilaterally truncated two-thirds of the land of Israel that Britain in the Balfour Declaration promised to the Jewish people, and was instead promising it to the Arabs. I felt it would lead to a conflict of interest to work with the younger Samuel. Samuel replied by saying that my command of the English language was surely good enough, and as far as my employment with the government was concerned, he would ask the high commissioner, Lord Gort, to send a letter to the head of my department requesting permission for me to accept the job. In that letter he would assure my department head that my job would not interfere with my official duties in the government. He told me I would not have to work on Shabbat and Jewish holidays; and he added that he, too, was a Zionist, a member of the Kibbutz Mishmar Hayarden, where he lived before his marriage. He did not react negatively to my aspirations to see the establishment of a Jewish state, nor did he express opposition to my ideals. As far as he was concerned, the four arguments that I presented did not justify my refusal. A week later, the High Commissioner sent a letter to the head of my department, Mr. Fletcher, recommending that I be permitted to work with Samuel in his tutorial classes. I could now look forward to the opportunity to train the civil service of the future Jewish state.

Building the political infrastructure of a new nation, even with other established nations to use as models, is no easy task. When your residents have fled persecution and the horrifying immediacy of threats to the lives of oneself and one's family, the difficulties are multiplied. And when one has escaped this frying pan *into* a situation when one's neighbors are actively shooting at you, the obstacles are astronomical to contemplate. Building a civil service to operate in war or peace to sustain the new nation was a good stiff challenge.

I was appointed chief registrar and secretary of the Jerusalem Tutorial Classes. Samuel arranged for me to share an office with the secretary general of the YMCA, across the street from the King David Hotel. I was allowed to work part time registering new students. Both Jews and Arabs enrolled in the tutorial classes. We had good teachers, including an American diplomatic representative who was the Consul of the United States in Jerusalem, Wells Stabler; Professor Raphael Patai, the first Ph.D. of the Hebrew University; and distinguished professors who lectured on administrative law and government institutions. One of these courses was given by Major Aubrey Eban, later known to the world as Abba Eban.

The Institute of Public Administration in Israel was an independent body concerned with providing training for public administration in its widest sense. This included post-entry training for government civil service, municipal service, public utilities, and the large industrial and commercial organizations. The Institute had been founded in 1947 by its then principal, the Honorable Edwin H. Samuel, as The Middle East College of Public Administration. It consisted of three component units: the Jerusalem Tutorial Classes, started in 1945, the Jerusalem Diploma Course in Public Administration, conducted in English for both Jewish and Arab students, and the Tel Aviv Tutorial Classes, with which I was to be associated, where courses were conducted in Hebrew.

The Jerusalem units suspended activities in 1948 during the catastrophic upheaval that accompanied the end of the Mandate and the Arab siege of Jerusalem, but was reopened in 1949 for Jewish students only. The Arabs left after the Jewish successful defense during the Arab siege. The Diploma Course in Public Administration was restarted in 1950 in Jerusalem and Tel Aviv. The first Tutorial Classes were then organized in Haifa. Those in Tel Aviv continued uninterruptedly from 1946 on. About 250 students were in training in the institute at any one time, mostly in three-month terms. The diploma course ran for eighteen months. A nine-month certificate course in Local Government was held in Tel Aviv in 1947 and was later repeated.

About eighty courses were offered at three centers—Jerusalem, Tel Aviv, and Haifa. Twelve hundred students passed through the institute, about one-third being civil servants; one-third, local government officers; and the remainder bank and public utility officials. Many students continued in class after class and in Tel Aviv the demand for places consistently exceeded our ability to supply them. These programs, in aggregate, provided the foundation of the Israeli civil service.

The participant population consisted of students in the 25-35 age range. There were more men than women. Most students had completed secondary schooling; a few had completed university, and there were even a few Ph.D.'s among the student body.

The curriculum was geared to the diverse levels of education among the students. Subjects studied were mostly in what was coming to be called the social sciences, divided into theoretical subjects (such as the theory of public administration, economics, statistics, psychology, sociology, history, law, and political science) and applied subjects (such as, for example, the natural resources of the Middle East, the administration of Israel, United States diplomatic history, British constitutional development). Languages, the arts, the sciences and commercial school subjects (such as stenography and accountancy) were not included, although there were peripheral courses from time to time on subjects such as Aesthetics or Science and the State.

The institute had a staff of twelve volunteer organizers,

nearly all of whom were public officials. Some organizers also acted as tutors, but most tutors were drawn as needed from the Hebrew University, the senior ranks of the central and local government staffs, or from among leading practitioners in the various professions.

The institute evolved into a state-aided institution and received an annual grant from the Israeli Ministry of Education. This grant covered its administrative expenditure, which was very small. The tutors' fees were covered by the students' tuition, which was also low. Much voluntary work was done by the students themselves, who were organized in a Students' Association in each of the three cities. The Students' Association elected its own chairman and supervisory board and included as members all past and present students. They helped the tutors with the distribution of material to the class, the collection of fees, the maintenance of the attendance register, and the organization of indoor entertainments such as film shows, guest lectures, concerts, visits, and tours. These multiple roles put demands on the students, but enhanced their level of participation—what in the public world would be called grass-roots participation—in ways that are now universally recognized as beneficial.

The institute attempted to fulfill the functions performed by similar institutes in the United States, Great Britain, France, and other countries. In general, it aimed at elevating the training and status of the governmental and nongovernmental administrator to that of a professional similar to a lawyer, doctor, or university teacher. The institute issued its own Hebrew quarterly journal of public administration under the name *Haminhal* (the

Hebrew term for Administration). The Israeli public's response to the journal was tremendously encouraging.

The institute had a public administration library, largely in English, and also published its own textbooks. The first, which appeared in 1947 in separate English and Hebrew editions, was on the theory of administration. Another, on administrative training methods, was added later.

As the governmental administration (some might say bureaucracy) developed, the institute was increasingly called in to consult on planning administrative training courses in other institutions. The program was widely recognized as successful, and as a result such courses were organized for secretaries-general from the different ministries in the arts of administrative planning and execution; for personnel officers in methods of training civil servants; for branch managers in the Anglo-Palestine Bank; for hospital administrators under the auspices of the Ministry of Health; for officials of the Ministry of Rationing and Supply; for officials of the Income Tax Department; and for the staffs of local authorities under the auspices of the League of Local Councils.

The institute further organized research groups to investigate a number of more important administrative problems that have faced Israel to this day. The field was vast, and every effort and assistance to improve the efficiency of the administration of Israel was welcomed.

The courses, given in the evening after regular business hours, twice a week, were well received by both the students and teachers. I enrolled in a course on British institutions tutored by Aubrey Eban. I had known Eban from my regular visits to bookstores in Jerusalem where he would browse regularly, always in his splendid army uniform. The Jewish community at the time was very small, and it seemed as if everyone in Jerusalem knew each other. Major Eban taught in the Middle East School for British Intelligence Officers in the Old City. At our first class, Eban delivered an excellent outline of his course on British institutions. I had never before heard a lecturer with such an extraordinary command of the English language. That same evening, I went to Samuel's home and told him how impressed I was with Eban's introduction. I almost facetiously suggested that, if Eban were only Jewish, he would make an outstanding spokesman for the Zionist cause. I had no idea, neither by his name nor by his appearance, that Eban *was* Jewish. Samuel looked at me with an odd smile on his lips and assured me that Eban was Jewish. I ran into Eban soon thereafter on several occasions at the YMCA building during the sessions of the Anglo-American Committee of Inquiry convened by the British government and the United States to recommend a solution to the Palestine problem.

These were tense days in Eretz Israel. The Jewish underground, consisting of the basic defensive force Haganah, the revisionist and more aggressive Irgun Tzv'ai Leumi (also known by the Hebrew acronym Etzel), and the Lechi (the militant Stern Group under the command of Itzhak Shamir, later prime minister of Israel) had become increasingly active when the British imposed new restrictions on Jewish immigration. The British government shut the portal to Palestine at the very time when thousands of survivors of the Holocaust in Europe sought to immigrate. The British knew that this situation was unacceptable and were looking for a way to disentangle themselves from their commitments in the Balfour Declaration. They began to realize that what Jabotinsky once said at the Zionist Congress had become the prevailing Jewish viewpoint: "the Balfour Declaration was not our Mandate, the Bible is our Mandate."

The realization by the British of a biblically-based and thus rock-solid Jewish intractability was what prompted the formation of the Anglo-American Committee of Inquiry. In the common translation of the Tanakh, the so-called Jewish Bible (the Old Testament to Christians) there are references to the Jews as being "a stiff-necked people." With our backs against the wall, we certainly are.

Later on, Eban also served as the liaison officer between the Jewish Agency and the United Nations Special Committee on Palestine, UNSCOP. I was pleased to see him in his official roles; he was such a brilliantly poised and eloquent diplomatic spokesman for the Jewish Agency.

Some of the other teachers in the Jerusalem Tutorial Classes were Norman Bentwich, whom we have met before as attorney general and obstructionist, now the head of the Reali School in Haifa; and a famous Arab historian, Professor Philip Hitti of Princeton University, who once wrote that there never was a "Palestinian" people nor a "Palestinian" state.

Two-thirds of the teachers were Jews, one-third were Arabs. We established a specialized library in public administration that eventually became the largest of its kind in the Middle East. Following the success of the tutorial classes in Jerusalem, tutorial classes were also organized in Tel Aviv. Gila Uriel, the very efficient secretary to the Mayor of Tel Aviv, was named principal of the Tel Aviv Tutorial Classes and directed a program that emphasized local government administration. Mrs. Uriel also published *Haminhal,* for the organization, a sizable contribution on its own.

In 1947, we organized a diploma course for the advanced study of public administration in Jerusalem. Of the twenty-five students admitted, all were graduates of the Hebrew University, the Jerusalem Law School, and the School of Economics in Tel Aviv. The diploma course was held in the same building where I had worked in the Department of the Custodian of Enemy Property. That branch of the government administered the property of alien countries that were in a state of war with England. We managed the assets of these aliens, including their holdings in real estate. I had a staff of about sixteen people, most of them Christian and Moslem Arabs. I appointed a Moslem as my assistant, and I worked in that department until the end of the mandatory administration.

For historic reasons, I wish to record an interesting account concerning future planning on the part of one of my close cousins, Mordecai HaLevi. Born Mordecai Turkel, he was a well-known and popular soccer player back in Vienna, playing for the HaKoach team.

HaLevi, who changed his name when he came to Israel just as we and many others did, to a more Hebraic name, had a unique hobby. He was also an aviator. In Palestine, during the British occupation, there was no airport in or near Jerusalem. We realized that when the British would pull out and leave, as we were confident they would, the newly formed State of Israel would need a landing field in Jerusalem so that our small forces (in comparison to the vastly outnumbering Arab forces, very small) could quickly shuttle between Jerusalem and Tel Aviv. Local bombing raids (our bombs then were mostly loud noise makers) could also be launched from Jerusalem if we had an airfield. The British, however, would never allow it. When the British finally did leave Palestine, they made sure to leave any remaining arms in the hands of the Arabs. Jews were forbidden to have weapons. The British projected a quick Jewish defeat to the inevitable Arab attack expected (by just about everyone) after they left. This would then require their prompt return to Palestine to re-establish peace and save what remaining lives they imagined might yet be left. At least, that was the word on the street regarding their hope and expectations. In any case, the British would not permit the Jews to prepare for the inevitable war for independence (i.e., survival) and that included any idea of preparing an airfield in Jerusalem. So what did my cousin do?

As a well-known soccer player, he was readily able to organize a soccer team in Jerusalem, and he directed the team and others, soccer fans mostly, to clear a field that was long and flat, of any and all obstacles such as rocks, shrubs, even trees. This of course was being done in the interests of the sport, to establish a field on which they could play. The British police, discovering the activity, inquired suspiciously as to what their purpose was in clearing such a large area. Mordecai HaLevi[9] explained

---

[9] HaLevi later founded and ran a successful travel company in Jerusalem called Travex.

how they had formed a soccer team and needed a large enough field on which to play, as well to hold some fans who might like to watch the games. The police permitted them to continue and even offered their assistance, out of the interest for the sport, of course. Thus, a small, debris-free airfield was prepared under the guise of a soccer field. HaLevi did organize some games there once the field was cleared, while the British remained in control, I believe. But the intent was the early preparation for an airfield, which played a somewhat important role during the war later. Mordecai HaLevi flew sorties from that tiny airstrip in a small piper airplane for both reconnaissance and bombing runs. (The bombings consisted of his reaching down between his legs and grabbing small noise-grenades one at a time and dropping them from the air as he flew above enemy-occupied territories.) Although it is highly doubtful he ever hit anything by just dropping these bottles out the side of his plane (beyond perhaps a particularly unlucky, stray scorpion scampering between two rocks), the loud blasts and the appearance of air—strike capabilities most certainly had favorable psychological effects on the enemy.

At one point, after the state was established, Golda Meir shuttled to Jerusalem, landing on that airstrip. Part of the field still serves as a playing arena for a Rechavia (area of Jerusalem) Gymnasium.

At the end of 1947, Mr. Ben-Gurion, then chairman of the Jewish Agency, asked the economic department to recommend alternate sources of income from the United States other than through the United Jewish Appeal. Dr. Josef Barrnea, deputy head of the department, who was my teacher in the diploma course of the Middle East College of Public Administration, asked Mr. Meiri, the comptroller of the Zionist Organization, and me to follow through on Ben-Gurion's request.

We made three suggestions, first, recommending an Israeli sweepstakes similar to the Irish sweepstakes, which, at the time annually brought in more than $70 million from the United States alone. Our second recommendation was to encourage the sale to Americans of second homes in Israel. Our third recommendation was to issue Israel Bonds at a reasonable rate of interest.

I was asked to inquire upon my impending arrival in the United States how we could implement these recommendations. Once in New York, I learned that the Irish sweepstakes were not legal, and I concluded that Israel, a new state, could not engage in an illicit project. As far as the sale of secondary homes was concerned, we learned that there was no great interest at the time among American Jews to acquire second homes in Israel. The third recommendation, Israel Bonds, remained our only alternative. I reported my findings to Israel and to the Israeli Development Bank in Geneva.

Mr. Ben-Gurion accepted our conclusion, dispatching Teddy Kollek to America to orchestrate the Israel Bond campaign. The first meeting, attended by some 5,000 American Jewish leaders, was held in the Armory in Washington, D.C., in the presence of Secretary of the Treasury, Henry J. Morgenthau, and Golda Meir as a representative of Israel. I was present at that meeting, which inaugurated the Israel Bond organization in the United States.

Despite the opposition of the United Jewish Appeal, headed by Mr. Montor, the Israel Bond organization developed rapidly, and its success defied the imagination of its founders because the strategy pursued was not for American Jews to be asked to *donate* money but rather to *invest* money that would give them a reasonable return. The Chase Manhattan Bank in New York accepted our offer to underwrite the bonds, the sale of which, to this date, has surpassed billions of dollars.

After the United Nations resolution of November 29, 1947, with Arabs rioting in the streets of Jerusalem, any trip to my office on the Mamilla Road close to the Old City became hazardous beyond imagination. I became increasingly committed to moving our invaluable library on public administration to a safer place. I thought that the library would be vital as an important source of reference in planning the administration of the future government of Israel and its various services. The National Library at the Hebrew University on Mount Scopus was equally inaccessible during the siege of Jerusalem, besides which it had only a limited number of books on public administration. The president of the university, Yehuda Magnes, as stated in a different context elsewhere, did not believe in a politically independent Jewish State in Eretz Israel and felt, therefore, no particular need for such a specialized library.

Since I was well known to my colleagues in the civil service, I asked the chief clerk of the Public Works Department to provide me with a truck and driver for the transfer of our books to the office of the chief secretary, at the King David. My colleague obliged, and we loaded the truck with books, office furniture, and bookshelves. I instructed the driver that, upon his arrival at the King David, he should park the truck in the street and immediately report to the Civil Service Commission on the upper floors of the hotel. Jerusalem was divided at that time into security zones that were separated by barbed wire. He did exactly as instructed.

When he later came down to the street to unload, however, he must have been dismayed to find the truck missing. He probably deduced that he forgot where he had parked it. In the meantime, by design, I had arranged for another driver to take over the truck in the first driver's absence and proceed from the King David Hotel in Security Zone A to the Jewish Agency building on King George Avenue in Security Zone B, across the street from my house. There I waited for him anxiously, in order to continue together to the Bezalel Museum, but not before a brief stop-over, during which we rapidly unloaded the books into my home for safekeeping and future access. We proceeded to the Bezalel Museum where we unloaded the furniture. Curiously, that museum had been co-founded by my cousin's husband, Abel Pann, who was surprised, to put it mildly, by the furniture's unexpected arrival. The empty truck was returned in good condition (to the driver's relief) to the Public Works Department.

When Edwin Samuel learned about this secretive operation (hardly my first), he came to my home to express his gratitude. In response to his request, I made all the resources of the college library available to Ze'ev Shaerf, a secretary to David Ben-Gurion, head of the Jewish Agency. Director General of the Foreign Ministry,

Walter Eytan, utilized the library as well in the establishment of the diplomatic service. I was later appointed assistant secretary and head of the Department of Administration and Personnel for the Ministry of Foreign Affairs under him.

Our library, as I thought it would, served its purpose mightily in the planning of the government of Israel, which was then being organized. Ze'ev Shaerf eventually became the Secretary of the Israeli Cabinet and our library proved to be an indispensable source of reference in organizing the government departments. The governmental departments were being put into operation on the pattern of the English and American bureaucracies. Naturally, we had to consider the special conditions in Israel, the size of the country, and its limited financial resources. In one particular instance we followed the example of the British Foreign Office, which maintained a branch, a representative office, in Southampton. At the foreign ministry we established a representative office in the port of Haifa, administered by Harry Beilin a former staff member of the Jewish Agency in Jerusalem.

When the personnel of the former Palestinian governing body left the country on April 14, 1948, one month before the declaration of Israel's independence, Edwin Samuel returned with them to England. His two sons, however, remained in Israel and served in the army. Before returning to England, Edwin Samuel authorized me to act in his absence as his representative in all private and personal matters.

During the War of Liberation, I was in a troop assigned to liberate the highlands of Katamon, which is now *inside* Jerusalem because the city has grown so much. We used Samuel's house as a staging ground from where we could shoot into Katamon, because it had a perfect view of the surrounding area. When we entered into Katamon, we found that the Arab residents had just fled, leaving their breakfasts still warm on the table.

As soon as the siege of Jerusalem was lifted, due to strong Jewish resistance, Edwin Samuel named me acting principal of the Jerusalem Tutorial Classes, whereupon I changed the name of the institution to the Israel Institute of Public Administration. The inaugural ceremony of the new institution was held at the Beit Hahalutz in Jerusalem, under the chairmanship of Professor Leo Cohen, an expert on constitutional law, who later served as a consultant to the Israel Ministry for Foreign Affairs.

The students in our diploma course had completed their studies just in time for the declaration of Israel's independence on May 15, 1948. I was deeply and lastingly gratified to have played a role in the training in public administration of some 1,800 students and of having helped to build the largest library on public administration in the Middle East.

After the United Nations vote on the partition of Palestine, the Arabs resorted to violence in Jerusalem, determined to undo that resolution. They burned the Rex Hotel on Queen Alessandra Road in the center of the city and attacked Jewish residents. To organize our defense, a group within the Jewish Agency associated with the Haganah formed the *Mishmar Ha'am* (civil guard of Jerusalem). Its members (of whom I was one) were called upon to undertake some of the municipal functions. In the event that civil war broke out, we planned to supply the population with water, food, and shelter. Members of the civil guard were also assigned to watch the buildings that were likely targets of Arab attacks. The civil guard gradually became a shadow administration of the municipality of Jerusalem. Its secretary general, appointed by the Jewish Agency, was a member of the Haganah, Mordecai Marcus Awiezer. He was a man beloved in my memory as one of the unrecognized heroes of the struggle.

Extra-special priority consideration had been given to the defense of Jerusalem. For this purpose, we launched a census of the population to familiarize ourselves with the locations and numbers of inhabitants in each building, so as to be able to find residents in the event of an explosion. To undertake this census, we assigned a renowned professor of statistics at the Hebrew University, an immigrant from Italy by the name of Professor Bachi, to conduct it. Our survey was performed under the most difficult conditions imaginable. The city was under siege and a target of Arab attacks from the surrounding hills. People were killed or wounded in the streets daily while lined up to receive a supply of water or when they ventured out to do essential shopping.

We conducted our survey from house to house and from room to room. The population was cooperative because they understood the need for the census for their own safety. The Jordanian Arab Legion, headed by British Colonel Glubb Pasha, killed and wounded many Jewish civilians in the streets, and Professor Bachi regrettably became one of his victims, killed while standing guard in front of the Orion cinema in Jerusalem.

While still in the civil guard, I was dispatched to the southernmost part of Israel. I arrived at Eilat to help secure the border there. Eilat is now a popular resort but did not exist then. There was no fresh water anywhere around, and the seawater was infested with sharks. When we reached the southern shore, I looked around and was awed and a bit frightened to realize I was only a few miles away from Aqaba in Jordan, which was clearly visible from there, across the sea's end.

Also visible, though, was the edge of the Sinai Mountains. It is a sight never to be forgotten. Every color of the rainbow is discernable there. The first night after we arrived, I slept on a huge, long stone (the size of a van) with a relatively flat top, which protruded from the sand near the shore.

Setting up a station there was also an unforgettable experience for an entirely different reason. Whoever was in charge of equipping our expedition neglected to provide us with any water. Our few jeeps and trucks were stocked with some food rations—and wine. In the hot desert landscape that surrounded us, wine was all we had with which to refresh ourselves, that is, until we managed to find a small Arab village a day or two later named Bier Hindis, (*Be'er Hahandassah*, in Hebrew, the "Well of the Engineers") where we were able to barter for some water.

On our return trip, I was privileged to ride together with Dr. Alexander Dotan in a covered jeep. Dr. Dotan was a renowned historian and archeologist. The jeep was equipped with a two-way radio, which came to life when someone blared anxiously from a Jerusalem office that the government had received apprehensive communiqués that we had violated Jordanian territory and had entered Aqaba. Unfettered, Dr. Dotan readily replied that we indeed had not. He said after a moment's thought that we were in Eilat and, of course, well within our own borders. This sent diplomats worldwide scurrying through their maps, looking for Eilat, which of course wasn't on any of them since there was nothing there but sand and sea (and some huge boulders). It was thus that Eilat sprang into being and got its name.

Within a short time, the Mishmar Ha'Am in Jerusalem expanded its services to include a Department of Water Supply, equipped with special trucks that were made available as soon as the water lines to Jerusalem were cut off. Water and food had to be rationed.

To illustrate the gravity of the siege of Jerusalem in a personal way, I recall an episode related to my grandmother, who came to visit from Tel Aviv. She was stranded in our home when Jerusalem was cut off from the rest of the country. Unable to return to Tel Aviv, she remained with us, fell sick and needed special nutritious food. I still have in my possession the certificate granting permission to buy one egg and a small chicken for my sick grandmother. The food supply was so short that people engaged in barter, exchanging a can of sardines for some other provisions. The civil guard was ordered to man the checkpoints that divided the security zones that the British established in the city, and was also charged to secure the safety of public institutions. These functions, a product of necessity, resulted in the maintenance of a city under siege until such time as the siege ended. At that point, the civil guard's responsibilities reverted to the local police authority.

During the long period of my association with Edwin Samuel, I met many of his guests at social gatherings at his home. Among them was the wife of the first president of Israel, Vera Weizmann; Lord Marks of the British firm of Marks and Spencer; the famous British philosopher Isaiah Berlin; Abba Eban; and, among others, Walter Eytan. A former don at Oxford University, Eytan was engaged by the Jewish Agency to establish a school for diplomats. He was keen about learning from our experience in the tutorial classes, and Edwin Samuel had asked me to assist him, which I did when I extended the use of the library to him. At that time I was wary regarding his school because I was sure that once the state was established, the diplomatic service would certainly be staffed by members of the Mapai, Israel's ruling party, to which I was opposed.

To the everlasting credit of Walter Eytan, when the ministry for foreign affairs was organized he remembered my assistance. When the siege of Jerusalem ended, I accompanied my grandmother on her return to Tel Aviv. I made an appointment to see Eytan at the offices of the foreign ministry, and following a pleasant conversation, I was offered a position as assistant secretary general of the ministry. I gladly accepted the serendipitous appointment, and assumed my duties one day before the arrival of its Secretary General, Chaim Radai. I was the eighth officer to be hired in the Foreign Ministry, and one of its first members to be charged with the responsibility of organizing Israel's diplomatic service. Hindsight grants this role even more significance than I realized at the time; I had been instrumental in the formation of a civil service, and now I was being charged with setting up the foreign service for my country.

My duties as Assistant Secretary General and its first Director of Personnel and Administration, called for the hiring of staff. Almost every day, countries around the world recognized Israel either *de jure* or *de facto*. We were eager to consolidate our position internationally by establishing representative offices in those countries. The principle that guided me in the selection of personnel was that appointments be based strictly on merit. I was reluctant to recommend officers merely because of their party affiliation, so I compiled a multi-dimensional questionnaire that every applicant had to complete. Many Israelis offered their services in the hope that by joining the Foreign Office they would be able to travel and see the world.

A questionnaire provided me with information on the applicant's education and his or her knowledge of languages, but did not give me an insight into the character and personality of the individual. It therefore became necessary to conduct personal interviews. Due to the shortage of food in the country, and the constant danger of warfare, as well as the eagerness of Israelis to travel around the world, hundreds of applicants asked for these interviews. In the absence of a statutory merit system, I had to rely on my judgment before recommending a candidate. There were no entrance exams. During my tenure—in fact within two years—I assisted in establishing forty-six diplomatic and consular offices and participated in the hiring of some six hundred people, men and women, and their supporting staff and the acquisition of the office equipment. I worked an average of eighteen hours a day with a staff of only three assistants and three secretaries.

One of our early missions was to be dispatched to Moscow. The Soviet Union, together with the United States, voted for the establishment of the Jewish state in Israel at the United Nations on November 29, 1947. Mrs. Golda Meir was appointed to be Israel's first envoy to the Soviet Union. Golda was born in Kiev, Ukraine, in 1898, and her family moved to Milwaukee, Wisconsin, in 1906, where she became a public school teacher. In 1921, she and her husband, Morris Meyerson, immigrated as *chalutzim* (pioneers) to Eretz Israel. Both were members of the Zionist Socialist Youth Organization. Throughout her stay in Israel she faced many difficulties as both a wife and a mother. Ultimately, Mr. and Mrs. Meyerson separated.

I would like to correct a false impression regarding Golda Meir's appointment as Israel's envoy to Moscow. In the United States it is commonly accepted that Golda Meir was sought out to fill this critical position. This was not truly how it happened. Neither Prime Minister Ben-Gurion nor Foreign Minister Sharett, each for his own reasons, was eager for Ms. Meir to serve as Israel's envoy to the Soviet Union. Golda Meir spent many days in my office actively and persistently campaigning for that assignment. The secretary general of the foreign ministry, my immediate superior, Chaim Radai (originally Chaim Berman), a former member of the staff of the Jewish Agency in Jerusalem, once served as Golda Meir's secretary in the Jewish Agency. Golda Meir spent several days pleading with Radai to use his influence with Foreign Minister Sharett and the Mapai party to endorse her appointment. Yitzhak Ben-Zvi and Zalman Shazar, future presidents of Israel, and Ehud Avriel (with whom I grew up in Vienna) were very close friends of Ms. Golda Meir. Avriel once served as the representative of the Haganah in Europe. When Israel achieved independence and found it difficult to find arms from other sources (America and Great Britain not being helpful), he was made Israel's first appointed ambassador, to Prague in Czechoslovakia. In that capacity, he was able to secure a supply of arms from that country. Golda Meir implored him to intercede on her behalf, and Ehud Avriel complied.

The Soviet envoy in Israel, Mr. Yershov, was asked what qualifications were required to ensure the success of an Israeli ambassador in his country. Was it required, he was asked, that the ambassador speak the Russian language? He responded that speaking Russian was certainly helpful but not absolutely essential. In his opinion Golda Meir was well suited for the position. In the course of time, Mr. Ben-Zvi and Mr. Shazar, Chaim Radai, and Ehud Avriel, all leaders of Mapai, convinced Prime Minister Ben-Gurion and Foreign Minister Sharett to appoint Golda Meir as Israel's "Envoy Extraordinaire and Minister Plenipotentiary" to Moscow, pro facto an ambassador.

Once her appointment was confirmed, I met with her almost daily in my office to brief her on the organizational chart that I had designed to ensure the communication of her legation with the Eastern European department in the Foreign Ministry that was responsible for the Russian Desk. It was my duty to establish smooth communication between our embassies and the foreign ministry.

Upon the accession of Golda Meir, we named Aryeh Levavi, an assistant head of our Eastern European department, to be the first secretary of our mission to the Soviet Union. Levavi later served as Israel's ambassador to Argentina at the time when Adolf Eichmann was captured in Buenos Aires. General Yohanan Ratner, a former professor at the Technion in Haifa, was named Israel's attaché. Mr. Mordechai Namir, who later became the mayor of Tel Aviv, served in the legation with the title of minister. Eiga Shapiro, whose husband, Moshe Medzini was a famous radio commentator in Israel, together with Mrs. Lou Kaddar, were appointed personal secretaries to Golda Meir. The entire Israeli mission in Moscow lived like a kibbutz in the Hotel Metropole, in Moscow, managing on a limited expense budget. They shared everything as a family.

Golda Meir was scheduled to arrive in Moscow shortly before Rosh Hashanah. I advised Foreign Minister Mr. Sharett that, considering that Russian Jewry had been cut off for thirty years from the currents of Jewish life, there was now an opportunity to feel the pulse to see whether the Jews of the Soviet Union were still attached to the Jewish people by asking Golda Meir to attend the synagogue in Moscow on Shabbat and the High Holidays. I said that I would arrange a whispering campaign to let the people know Golda Meir would attend services in the synagogue. If the people then came to pray in the synagogue, it would demonstrate clearly that Russian Jewry was still very much alive and interested in its link with their Jewish past and tradition. For all that, I was doubtful whether Sharett and Golda Meir would agree to my suggestion as neither was known to be an observant Jew.

To my surprise, both Sharett and Golda Meir graciously accepted the suggestion. Sharett, however, took me aside and told me that he doubted whether the synagogue in Moscow had even so much as a Torah scroll or prayer books, or any other religious articles required for the services on Shabbat and the High Holidays. Following that conversation, I made an appointment to meet the president of the Great Synagogue on Allenby Street in Tel Aviv, Mr. David Tzvi Pinkas, a co-signer of Israel's Declaration of Independence, who was also a native of Vienna and a schoolmate of mine. I asked him if he could supply a Torah scroll, prayer books, and a shofar and other religious articles that we wished to send to our legation in Moscow.

This request was granted within a week. To ensure that the baggage would not be opened by Russian customs officials and that the religious articles contained therein were not to be confiscated, the crates were clearly marked as being diplomatic property. After the British administration left Palestine, we used French instead of English as our second language after Hebrew. It was a highly emotional moment for me to see all these religious articles being packed in crates and marked "*Etat d'Israel, Baggage Diplomatique*" ("State of Israel, Diplomatic Baggage").

I sent two planes to Moscow. One preceded the arrival of Golda Meir. It contained the office equipment, files, stationery, passports, and visa stamps. It also brought in its luggage section underneath a crate with religious articles. A second plane arrived carrying Meir and her staff.

A few days before her arrival a famous Russian Jewish author and journalist, Ilya Ehrenberg, wrote an article in the Communist Party newspaper *Pravda* in which he made veiled threats to Russian Jews that they should refrain from dealing with Israel and declare themselves loyal Russian citizens only. He demanded that the Russian Jews emphasize how fortunate they were to live in the Soviet Union. They should not go out of their way to associate themselves with Israel. The Russian Jews did not lend credence to this.

One Shabbat, soon after Ms. Meir arrived in Moscow, she went to the synagogue with the entire legation. Only a small number of people attended the prayer service. When she told the congregation that she would come to the synagogue again on the High Holidays, the announcement reverberated among Moscow's Jews. On Rosh Hashanah, dressed in a white gown, Golda Meir, together with the entire Israeli legation, attended the services in the synagogue. It was estimated that some 50,000 Jews lined the streets outside the synagogue, waiting for the opportunity to catch a glimpse of Israel's envoy and even to touch her. Some approached her in the Yiddish language, feeling overwhelmed, as if the Messiah himself had arrived in their midst. It was a uniquely poignant experience for Russian Jews to know that the State of Israel was now officially represented in the Soviet Union and accorded the same diplomatic privileges as all other nations. Israel was finally being accepted as an equal among equals.

That was exactly what I had in mind when I suggested to Foreign Minister Sharett that Golda Meir and the Israeli legation attend the services on Shabbat and the High Holidays in the Moscow synagogue. We concluded that there was still hope to see the redemption of Russian

Jewry in our days, and we were now convinced that the immigration of Russian Jews to Israel was attainable.

Ben-Gurion and Sharett were pleased with Golda Meir's visit and the Israeli legation to the Moscow synagogue. The visit, however, caused a sharp reaction by the Soviet government and had grave repercussions. The Jewish Theater in Moscow was closed by Soviet officials, and Jewish cultural life, as little as it existed, was brought to a complete halt. The identification of Russian Jews with their religion and with their people was explicitly discouraged. In short, Jews had to pay a heavy price for their short-lived expression of solidarity and identity. Israeli Jews' freedom to act and contact their family or co-religionists in the Soviet Union was restricted. Despite that communist enmity, Golda Meir, much to her credit, continued to go to the synagogue, and attend services during her entire stay in the Soviet capital.

During this time, Russian Jews could not discourage Soviet oppression. For practicing their religion, many Jews were sent to Siberia to their deaths, although individual refuseniks showed great heroism to keep the hope of redemption alive. It is to be regretted that one can never speak truthfully of any organized Jewish resistance in the Soviet Union. That was as impossible as it would have been in Nazi Germany. It is, though, true that, here and there, there were a few people and a few groups that staged some resistance to Soviet heavy-handedness.

After the demise of Stalin in the mid-1950s and the breakdown three decades later of the Soviet empire, a mass emigration of Soviet Jews to Israel demonstrated the ability of the Jewish people to survive against improbable odds. It proved that *Am Yisrael Chai,* the Jewish nation, lives on.

A singular incident happened during Golda Meir's tenure in the Soviet Union that tarnished Soviet-Israeli relations, and illustrates the severity of the Stalinist regime at the time. After Ms. Meir presented her credentials to Soviet Foreign Minister Vyacheslav Molotov, the minister hosted a large reception in her honor. In the course of this gathering, his wife, Pauline Zhemthuzhina Molotov, approached and spoke to Golda Meir in Yiddish, mentioning to her that she, too, was a *Yiddisheh tochter,* a Jewish daughter. Apparently the conversation was overheard by some Communist Party agents, after which, Mrs. Molotov was exiled to Siberia and was not heard from until after Stalin's death. Her husband, the foreign minister, had not interfered on her behalf to request her return to Moscow until the risk of doing so was removed, although they eventually reunited. In his memoirs, written after the death of Stalin, Andrei Gromyko alluded to her disappearance, but not in great detail. Upon returning from Moscow, Golda Meir became Israel's minister of labor, later succeeding Sharett as foreign minister, and she became prime minister in 1969. While prime minister, she and Eliahu Sassoon of the foreign ministry often met secretly with King Abdallah of Jordan to discuss the possibility of peaceful relations with Israel. Abdallah, a progressive when compared to other Arab leaders, or, for that matter, to British officers fulfilling that role (such as Glubb Pasha) nevertheless was nonplussed discussing matters of such weight with a woman, and a strong woman at that! King Abdallah was later assassinated by Arab extremists, as was Egyptian president Anwar Sadat some years afterward.

Just prior to the Yom Kippur War in 1973, while Golda Meir was serving as Israel's prime minister, U.S. Secretary of State Henry Kissinger warned her against launching a pre-emptive strike to counter Egypt's military build-up. Later, when she asked him for assistance, Kissinger's infamous answer was loud and unmistakably clear. He said that America, although a friend of Israel, was also a friend of the Arabs. He strongly asserted that he was an American first, secretary of state second, and a Jew third. Golda Meir calmly but futilely reminded him that, in Hebrew, we read from right to left. It was due primarily to President Richard M. Nixon, not to his ranking cabinet member, that Israel received the airplanes it so desperately needed to resist and ultimately defeat the Egyptian army.

Israel's foreign minister, Moshe Shertok, complimented my good judgment in the selection of personnel. It has always been my intention to further the careers of employees who worked for me. Some of my staff were ultimately appointed to hold responsible positions abroad: one of my assistants became ambassador to France, another was appointed first secretary in our embassy in London, while still others held important positions in our legations throughout the world. Among the foreign personnel I hired was Joseph Tekoah, who was recommended to me by Abba Eban. Tekoah was a graduate of Harvard University who became assistant legal advisor to the foreign ministry and Israel's permanent representative in the United

Nations, holding the rank of ambassador. At the time of his death he was president of Ben-Gurion University in the Negev. I was instructed to submit all applications for employment to a security officer in the foreign ministry, whose function was to check the credentials of prospective candidates. He simply marked on the corner of the application either "approved" or "denied." As a matter of principle, I did not wish to interfere in these security checks that were carried out by trained intelligence officers. In one special case, however, I was curious to know why an applicant was denied employment. The applicant, a former coloratura in the Tel Aviv Opera, had recently lost her husband, who had also been her accompanist at concerts. They had been on the way to the annual music festival in Ein-Gev. Crossing Lake Tiberias, the boat capsized, and her husband literally drowned in her arms. Heartbroken, she abandoned her career.

When she learned that a legation was established in Rome, she was interested to work there and use that opportunity to advance her vocal training in Italy. I could not understand why her application was denied. It was one of the few instances where I felt it necessary to inquire. The officer in charge of the security screening was the head of our code department and a good friend of mine. He revealed that in checking into her past it was discovered that when she was sixteen she had a boyfriend who was a member of the Irgun Tzv'ai Leumi. I clenched my teeth to remain silent because few of my colleagues knew that I was a member of the Irgun, a fact that had probably escaped the attention of our vigilant intelligence when I was first hired. I was outraged by the rejection of this qualified applicant, who in my opinion had all the requirements to serve honorably as secretary in our legation in Rome. Our envoy in Rome was a renowned lawyer, the son of Ahad Ha'am, one of the most outstanding Hebrew writers and philosophers. I was so outraged by the denial of that application that I brought this case directly to the attention of Foreign Minister Shertok. I told Shertok that I could not understand how this young lady, now serving as the secretary to the minister of justice, who had suffered a profound personal tragedy, should be declined employment only because she allegedly had a boyfriend in the Irgun when she was a young girl. Mr. Shertok did not favor me with a response.

During my government service, I came to know Shertok better, before and after he changed his name to Sharett. He was once the head of the political department of the Jewish Agency, and was an outstanding Hebraist, although pedantic in his manner. Despite this detachment, he had the exemplary qualities of a good teacher. He demanded that the officers and other officials adopt Hebrew names, though he himself had not yet done so.

When Shertok returned from the United Nations after its historic resolution of November 29, 1947, I organized a surprise welcome reception, which was attended by all the members of the staff of the foreign ministry and many ministers of the government and a great number of civil servants. A few days later, a meeting was held in my office under the chairmanship of Mr. Shertok. Pinchas Rosenbluth, the minister of justice, was also present.

It was a short time before the elections to the Knesset (Parliament) in Israel, and in his opening remarks, Shertok used the opportunity to impress upon the guests the need to adopt Hebrew names. Welcoming the minister of justice, he said that he hoped that after the elections his (the Minister's) name would be a different one. A native of Germany, Mr. Rosenbluth did not understand the humor of his suggestion, and took it instead as a personal insult, a call for his replacement. Barely concealing his irritation, he asked how Shertok already knew the results of the upcoming election. The solemnity of the occasion was interrupted by hilarious laughter at this misunderstanding.

I had another opportunity to gain some insight into the personality of Mr. Shertok, when, one day, he decided to remove his most devoted private secretary, Joseph Alon, a former classmate in the Herzliya Gynasium in Tel Aviv. He was not satisfied with the service of this man. I knew Alon to be a most dedicated and hardworking personal secretary. Shertok asked me, as head of the personnel department, to replace him, suggesting in the process a devious idea: that he would appoint Mr. Alon to another position within the foreign ministry, in a new department to be established for tourism. He felt that tourism, dealing with foreign countries, should be part of the foreign ministry. Once Mr. Alon was appointed to that position, Sharett assumed he would naturally ask for an appropriate budget to run his department. When that time came, Mr. Sharett said, he would deny Alon's request for funds. By this scheme he believed Mr. Alon would resign on his own initiative. Politics was deepening in Zion.

Yet another episode led me to start contemplating my future in the foreign service. An auxiliary police officer complained to the security services that, as a former

member of the Shomer Hazair in Vienna, a radical socialist movement, he could not understand how a leader of
the Betar movement in Vienna, referring to myself, could
serve in a senior position in the foreign ministry.
Following that denunciation, members of the internal
intelligence visited my office, and searched my desk draw-
ers for any suspicious articles. I had received an inkling of
such an action being perpetrated from the talk of colleagues in other departments, so when the intelligence
officers came to my office, they found nothing in my desk
other than some questionable literature that I had planted
there. I wanted to exacerbate their confusion, and had
always been a bit of a practical joker.

Another incident that aroused some indignation in me
involved the scheduling of meetings of the Mapai Party
within the foreign ministry's building. I felt "political meetings" should not be held inside a government office, and I
therefore brought this to the attention of the foreign minister. Shertok, himself a leading member of the Mapai,
rejected my complaint quite capriciously. Our working
relationship had again not ensured a mature, conscientious
responsiveness on his part. Was it personal or factional?

During my tenure, I endeavored to provide in-service
training for our staff. Weekly meetings were arranged
with our foreign representatives whenever they came to
Israel on their sojourn. The lecturers included ambassador to the United Nations, Abba Eban; the director general of the foreign ministry, Walter Eytan; and diplomatic
representatives of Poland, Czechoslovakia, and many
Latin American countries. In celebration of Jewish festivals and other occasions, I organized social gatherings to

strengthen the *esprit de corps*. These gatherings were also attended by the foreign minister and senior officers from other ministries.

To assure efficient communication between our foreign representatives and the geographical desk, I designed an organization chart, the one I had shown Golda Meir that illustrated the chain of command. Each envoy had to report to his respective geographical desk about his meetings and activities. Some of these reports were exceptionally revealing, and others were curious or even humorous. For example, in a memorandum from our ambassador to the Court of St. James in London, Mordecai Eliash reported that after he submitted his credentials to King George VI they met privately and during their conversation, King George asked the Envoy to explain the meaning of the Star of David. Mr. Eliash, a brilliant lawyer and scholar, had no difficulty enlightening the English monarch. The *Mogen David* (the Jewish Star) is composed of the interlocking of two triangles, a graphic representation of the letters in the name David, the first King of Israel. It has as a result become a symbol of the entirety of the Jewish experience, and is still revered accordingly by Jews around the world.

Another report came from our ambassador to Argentina, Jacob Tsur, who described how the president of that country, Juan Peron, as protocol required, sent his own personal carriage to bring him to his office for the presentation of his credentials. When the carriage arrived, Mr. Tsur found it difficult to believe his eyes when he saw that the carriage was drawn by four horses. Four was more than he expected.

Another occurrence was reported by Israel's first ambassador to Czechoslovakia, Ehud Avriel. We had no experience in the diplomatic procedures involved and copied verbatim for Avriel a letter of credentials that we had borrowed from the Dutch Consul General in Jerusalem. The government of Czechoslovakia returned the document to Avriel, with the remark that it was not acceptable. The Czech Chief of Protocol advised us that the credential Ambassador Avriel presented was only appropriate for a Consul and not for an envoy at the rank of ambassador. He supplied us with a sample of a letter of credential that another foreign ambassador had presented to his government. We copied that one, filled in the blanks, and Mr. Avriel was duly accredited. Thus, detail by detail, do organizations develop. In those days, the government of Czechoslovakia was uniformly friendly and helpful to Israel. Ehud Avriel, as stated before, secured many of the armaments required by the Israeli Defense Forces, which could not be obtained elsewhere. We were building a nation by the seat of our pants.

The Israeli division of administration and personnel included a section for protocol, headed by Ernst Simon. When he assumed that position, upon his arrival from Jerusalem, where he had served in the army, he immediately began to study diplomatic protocol. While doing so, he relied primarily on books written for the use of the German army and navy. Still dressed in army shorts, he came to Tel Aviv holding a top hat in his hand, ready for his new position. When he asked a salesman in a Tel Aviv department store to sell him three gloves, the salesman inquired why he would need three gloves. Simon responded that he needed the third glove because he had seen diplomats holding a glove in their hand, when in fact they had only taken off their right glove, holding it in their left hand, while shaking hands, as is proper, with a bare right hand.

IN HIS book *Altneuland*, Dr. Theodor Herzl quipped that the first president of Israel would be half blind, because in his opinion only a very learned scholar, who in the course of time had lost his good eyesight, could be elected as president of the Jewish state. The first president of Israel, Dr. Chaim Weizmann, arrived in Haifa from Geneva, where he had received medical treatment for what else?—an eye ailment. Upon his arrival, Mr. Simon ordered the navy to fire twenty-one salvos as a welcome to the president. He had no way of knowing that the navy was not equipped with a sufficient number of guns to fire that salute. However, to comply with the suggested protocol, the navy mounted regular cannons on deck. With every shot fired, the shell ricocheted back into the harbor. To recover it, the boat had to return to sea, and the firing had to start all over again. By the time the cannons in Haifa Harbor were still completing their twenty-one gun salute, the new president was probably fast asleep at his home in Rehovot.

It was my assignment to receive the first foreign diplomatic representative in Israel, Ambassador Yershov from the Soviet Union. One evening, I was still in my office when our representative, Harry Beilin, called from Haifa to say: "the Russians are here." Not understanding what he meant, I facetiously responded, "keep them there."

Beilin said the Russian delegation arrived at Haifa without prior notification, bringing their entire entourage and office equipment. Beilin alerted me that the legation was eager to proceed immediately to the Hotel Gat Rimon on Yarkon Street in Tel Aviv, where we arranged their accommodations. When I received this message I called my superior, Walter Eytan, for instructions. Eytan requested that I call on the legal advisor, Shabtai Rosenne, and Aryeh Levavi, Assistant to the Head of our Eastern European department, to join me in front of the hotel where we three should form a welcoming committee. Eytan concluded his instruction by saying that he wanted us to give the Russian diplomatic delegation, the first one to arrive in the State of Israel, a spontaneous reception, thereby expressing our gratitude for their vote in the United Nations favoring the establishment of the State of Israel.

I did as instructed and called on my three colleagues to come to the hotel immediately and wait for the arrival of the Russian diplomatic mission. However, I found it difficult to cope with Eytan's request for a spontaneous reception. My first thought was to go to Beth Brenner, the headquarters of the Mapai in Tel Aviv, and invite all the leftists there to greet the Russian envoy, with whose socialist ideas they no doubt identified. I decided, on second thought, that I would prefer to call on my good friend, Captain Eliezer Waldman, of the Israeli military police in Jaffa, to suggest (for security reasons) that he order the police to clear the street of all cars parked in front of the hotel. Only pedestrians should be allowed to assemble there.

Remembering the curiosity of the Viennese two

decades before who, at the slightest change of routine, would frantically rush from all corners to find out what was going on, I assumed that once the passersby in Tel Aviv heard Hayarkon Street was being closed they, too, would be curious to find out what was happening and come running. My conclusion, derived from Viennese experience, proved right on target. When I arrived soon thereafter in the official car of the foreign ministry displaying the blue and white flag, the military police on Ben Yehuda Street prohibited me from proceeding. All my protestations that I was on duty and all the identification papers presented to them did not help. The military police ordered me to walk one block to the hotel, where my colleagues were already waiting. Our welcoming party of three stood on the stairs of the hotel for over three hours expecting the arrival of the Russian convoy. The crowd grew as the evening wore on. It was already midnight when the cars and trucks finally arrived. Fortunately, the blackout in Tel Aviv, which was still in force in the afternoon, was suddenly lifted and the streets of Tel Aviv were illuminated. While waiting on the staircase of the hotel, I looked into the crowd and noticed my mother standing in the crowd. She had come to Tel Aviv that afternoon to visit her mother and had not had time to inform me that she would be there. I rushed to meet her, expressing my surprise that she did not wave to me, when she surely must have seen me. She replied that she did not feel it appropriate to disturb me while I was there on official business. Only a mother can act with such compassion or with such pride, in this case masquerading as humility.

When the Russian delegation at last arrived I greeted

Mr. Yershov with a friendly handshake. The only word I had learned in Russian from my colleagues was "*gaspudin*," meaning "sir," or "Comrade." I could not greet the Russian minister by repeating *gaspudin* all the time, so I smiled into the cameras of the press photographers who had assembled in front of the hotel. The Russian envoy Mr. Yershov did not respond to the warm welcome we extended to him. He asked to be ushered directly to his suite and only after he had checked the furniture, the upholstery, and the pictures on the wall for hidden microphones did he acknowledge our presence with some degree of human warmth.

Having already gained experience in receiving foreign diplomats, I was assigned to accompany our chief of protocol at the arrival of America's first representative, James MacDonald, a former High Commissioner for Refugees in the League of Nations. We arranged that the representatives of both the Soviet Union and the United States would be lodged in the same hotel to show our appreciation for their common "yes" votes on Israeli independent statehood, in the United Nations. America had not yet extended its *de jure* recognition of Israel and so Mr. MacDonald was named as the interim permanent representative of the United States of America to the provisional government of Israel, an extremely tentative and qualified designation, but a useful one.

I recall something that occurred immediately prior to MacDonald's arrival, when I discovered that the American flag had inexplicably been removed from its flagpole on the roof of the hotel while the Russian flag remained. We had instructed the management of the Gat

Rimon to hoist both flags, adjacent to each other, and that had somehow gone awry. When I noticed the American flag missing, I feared grave diplomatic repercussions as a result. I rushed to the hotel lobby, where I found a hotel waiter with a needle and thread in his hands repairing the American flag, which apparently had ripped. I reprimanded the waiters for not having found a more convenient time to do the repair than just minutes before the arrival of the American diplomat. The Stars and Stripes was immediately returned to its place, and Mr. MacDonald had no reason to be aware of its temporary absence.

MacDonald was accompanied by his daughter when he arrived in Israel. His first question when he stepped out of his car was to inquire in all sincerity about the well-being of Ben-Gurion and Golda Meir. Entering the hotel, one of the Israeli journalists with typical chutzpah asked him whether he would respond to a "diplomatic question." MacDonald answered that he knew of no diplomatic questions, only diplomatic answers. In contrast to the Russian envoy, MacDonald did not search for hidden microphones when he entered his suite. He was a man of a different sort, and from a country of a different nature.

MacDonald endeared himself to the Israeli public as far back as the time when he had served on the Anglo-American Committee of Inquiry and demonstrated his sympathy with Zionist aspirations. At the parade of the Israeli army on Israel's first Independence Day, MacDonald was on the reviewing stand next to Prime Minister Ben-Gurion and Soviet Minister Yershov. The

Israeli army was scheduled to pass by at exactly five o'clock in the afternoon. At that hour, unfortunately, no member of the Israeli army could be seen anywhere on the horizon. Since this was our first major parade, Israel was anxious about leaving a good impression on the foreign representatives, Ben-Gurion showed noticeable embarrassment when explaining, red-faced, the situation to the American envoy.

Suddenly a military police officer on a motorcycle drove up to the grandstand and reported that the march of the Israeli army was held up on Allenby, at the corner of Nachlat Benyamin Street, only a few blocks away. The masses of spectators could not be dispersed peaceably to allow the army to proceed. Noticing Ben-Gurion's discomfort, Mr. MacDonald, a tall person, leaned over to the much shorter Ben-Gurion and remarked humorously, "Mr. Prime Minister, the only people against whom the Israeli army can never win are the Jewish people," MacDonald in an instant diplomatically defused what might otherwise have been an awkward few minutes. When the Israeli army appeared on the parade route, everybody applauded what we then recognized was its winning over the citizens of Tel Aviv.

The first dinner for foreign diplomats given by the foreign minister and prime minister took place in the Dan Hotel in Herzliya. Our chief of protocol, Mr. Ernst Simon, strongly instructed the staff of the Foreign Ministry to be on their best behavior, and how to use the cutlery properly. The menu that evening, as it turned out, included chicken on the bone. In compliance with Simon's request, some dinner guests, with lifetimes of experience using their hands, tried to carve the chicken by using fork and knife. Soon the bones and pieces of meat observed the laws of physics and could be seen flying over the heads of the startled guests, propelled by a knife slipping on a chicken bone. To make a joke, it was then that the Israelis invented the boneless chicken breast!

The first diplomatic reception hosted by a foreign legation was given by the Soviet representatives at the Russian Embassy on Rothschild Boulevard in Tel Aviv. The party was attended by members of the Foreign Ministry, together with the president of Israel, Dr. Chaim Weizmann, members of the cabinet, and an extremely distinguished roster of guests. In those days, when everyone felt the scarcity of food, the Russians served a lavish menu including exotic fruits and pastry prepared by kosher caterers. After two hours, when the guests left the party, I was astonished to see that the quantity of food on the table seemed unchanged, not diminished, from the time we first arrived. I inquired about this phenomenon and the secretary of the Soviet delegation explained that it was the custom at Russian diplomatic parties not to let the guests feel that they had taken anything. The Soviet delegation did not always manifest this kind of courtesy. When one of their female secretaries took a liking to an Israeli boy, she was suddenly whisked away without any explanation on a Russian ship that had just entered the Haifa Harbor unannounced.

At the end of the War of Independence, a conference was held on the Greek island of Rhodes, under the auspices of the United Nations, to negotiate the armistice between Israel and Egypt. Ralph Bunche, the United Nations representative at this conference, who had once been an assistant to the late Count Folke Bernadotte, stood by to facilitate the agreement. The protocols of the negotiations were dispatched back and forth from Rhodes to Tel Aviv. I recruited officers to serve as couriers, and also volunteered myself for this assignment. With documents strapped to my hand, I boarded a United Nations plane that flew me from Haifa to the island of Rhodes.

Hours before the plane's departure, our representative in Haifa, Harry Beilin, asked me to attend a historic occasion, the return of the last group of "illegal" immigrants from Cyprus, who were detained there by the British army. I gladly accepted his offer to watch with him their arrival on the grandstand. All the boats in Haifa harbor were decorated with flags and sprayed water hoses to celebrate this occasion. There was a supremely festive atmosphere reminiscent of the holiday of Simchat Torah in a Hassidic synagogue, a scene of euphoria and ecstasy. While watching, I remembered the first boat of "clandestine" immigrants[10] I had organized a decade or so before, when the boat arrived in Haifa and the electricity in the harbor was short-circuited to cause a blackout so as to facilitate their landing. These immigrants who had been detained on Cyprus had been part of the original plan, and were now being repatriated, or, more correctly, patriated. This was a very emotional moment for me.

---

[10] See Chart in Appendix B.

While I was seated on the grandstand, a messenger came and informed me that my dear uncle Aaron Vardi in Tel Aviv had passed away and, consistent with Jewish tradition, the funeral was scheduled to take place that same afternoon. This uncle was the director of the Anglo-Palestine Bank who arranged for my parents to receive the certificates of immigration that saved their lives. As a Cohen I am not permitted to enter a cemetery, and so, with a heavy heart, not being able to attend the burial, I decided to board the United Nations plane to Rhodes. In Rhodes, I was accommodated in a very beautiful hotel that the Italians built during their occupation, the Hotel of the Roses. It was elegant, spacious, and extraordinarily comfortable; I was grateful.

A Jewish family in Rhodes invited me to their home and gave me a tour of that beautiful island. I saw many Jewish homes displaying mezuzahs on their entrances, although the houses lay in near-ruins as a result of the Nazi occupation during World War II. The generous hospitality extended by the Jewish population on that Greek island afforded an opportunity for me to relax from the trying conditions in Israel at the time.

Concluding two years of service in the foreign ministry, I was exhausted and required rest and recuperation. I took sick leave and returned home to Jerusalem, where I was placed under the care of Professor Herman Zondek, a prominent doctor, who ordered me to rest and remain under his observation for two weeks. After I recovered, I returned to my office in Tel Aviv. Opening the door to my office, I noticed a strange figure sitting at my desk. When I inquired about the reason for his presence, I was told that

ABOVE LEFT: Professor Milton Friedman, world famous economist, and Mordecai discussing solutions to Israel's economic problems.

ABOVE RIGHT: General Haig was very supportive of Mordecai's ideas and efforts in establishing the National Committee on American Foreign Policy.

Mordecai's opening remarks at the Symposium of the National Committee on American Foreign Policy in Washington, D.C. Secretary Joseph Cisco and Professor Hans Morgenthau are in attendance.

Mordecai with Professor Moshe Mandelbaum, Governor of the Bank of Israel, at one of the symposia.

When Mr. Kissinger spoke, everyone listened. Here on an auspicious occasion, Mordecai is speaking and Henry Kissinger is listening.

Mordecai with U.S. Congressman Jack Kemp, a staunch supporter of Israel as an important ally of the U.S.

BELOW: Best known as the father of the Hydrogen Bomb, Dr. Edward Teller was a frequent participant in Mordecai's symposia. Pictured here at the symposium introducing world class Russian scientists, such as the inventor of Sputnik, who had emigrated to Israel.

TOP LEFT: At a symposium of the American Israel Economic Corporation, Admiral Elmo Zumwald stressed the importance of Israel as an ally to the United States.

TOP RIGHT: In good company! Mordecai with great friends of Israel: Admiral Elmo Zumwalt, Patrick Moynihan, and a future President of Israel, Chaim Herzog.

LEFT: Senator Hubert Humphrey was a great American and a true friend of Israel. Pictured here at a rally with Mordecai, Rabbi and Mrs. Kirschblum, and Rabbi Emanuel Jacobowitz.

LEFT: Mordecai and his dear friend, John Loeb, U.S. Ambassador to Denmark.

RIGHT: Mordecai and the president of Bank Leumi New York, David Novick, being greeted by Mayor Ed Koch at Gracie Mansion.

Benyamin (Bibi) Netanhayu and
Mordecai shared many ideals and ideas,
and Bibi often looked to Mordecai as an
elder statesman.

BELOW: Mordecai and Prime Minister
Yitzhak Shamir, who had put his life on
the line fighting for Jewish independence
in Israel as the leader of the Lechi.

TOP: Mordecai and Hoshanah Hacohen with Israel's Prime Minister Menachem Begin and his wife, Aliza.

ABOVE LEFT: Mordecai receiving the Jabotinsky Medal from Prime Minister Menachem Begin.
ABOVE RIGHT: Mordecai with Vice President George H.W. Bush at his meeting with the Jewish Republican advisory committee. When Mordecai asked why the United States had not yet pressured the UN to declassify WWII war crimes records, the Vice President took out a small notebook and promised to follow up and inquire.

Otto and Mrs. Preminger with Mordecai and
Hoshanah Hacohen. The producer of the movie
Exodus was always excited to talk to Mordecai
about his personal experiences and real life adventures breaking the British blockade.

ABOVE: Mordecai with Presidents
Gerald Ford and Jimmy Carter at a
gala celebration of Admiral Hyman
Rickover's 80th Birthday in
Washington, D.C.

BELOW: Mordecai and long time
friend Harry Hurwitz, editor of the
South American Jewish Herald, shared
the same views and commitment to
the growth and flourishing of Eretz
Yisrael.

Professor and Mrs. Elie Wiesel, Dr. Steven Weiss, and
Mordecai attending a function in support of the State
of Israel.

Mordecai with the famous Nazi-hunter Simon
Wiesenthal.

The Kepicinitzer Rebbe bestowing a blessing upon Mordecai.

Mordecai and his son, Israel, receiving the blessing of Rabbi Shnerson, the Lubavitcher Rebbe.

RIGHT: Mordecai's and Hoshanah's engagement photograph.

BELOW: Mordecai introducing his sons, Israel and Ariel, to Shai Agnon, Israel's Nobel Prize laureate in literature.

BOTTOM LEFT: Mordecai and Hoshanah surrounded by their grandchildren.

BELOW: Mordecai skiing in St. Moritz.

in my absence Rechavam Amir was appointed to assume my duties. I found it strange that I was replaced during my short illness as if the foreign minister concluded that I would not recover or for some other reason not return. In answer to my queries, Mr. Sharett, Abba Eban, and Golda Meir, gave me evasive responses. I was also disappointed by the registrar of the prime minister's office, Chana Even Tov, who headed a committee of oversight of all government departments where I had served as a consultant. I must have made some waves in the corridors of the government because one day the head of the Western European Department, Gershon Avner, a member of Mapai, who seemed to be envious of my position, warned me to stop my complaints. If I failed to do so I would be sent to a remote area in the Negev not to be heard from for a long time. Administratively, the Negev was the political equivalent of Israel's Siberia.

My disappointment and disillusionment was so great that I then lost any trace of interest in my service with the foreign ministry. I had given all I could in the fight for the establishment of the State of Israel, the rescue of European Jews in the clandestine immigration, the defense of Jerusalem, the planning of the government departments, and my assistance in the service in the prime minister's office in the establishment of an efficient administration. I had not completed my studies for an advanced degree, I was single, and saw no prospects for any meaningful future in government service. Mapai's exclusivity was demonstrably clear, and Irgunists like myself would soon have no place at all in the government. Enough was enough. I felt it was time to move on. I was single and felt would do better for myself and for the State of Israel if I left for America.

In this mood, I recalled an incident in the 1930s that was the subject of one of Jabotinsky's speeches. It dealt with the trial of three Jews—Abba Achimeir (a former associate of Meir Grossman, founder of a Revisionist splinter group), Abraham Stavsky, and Zvi Rosenblatt—who were wrongly accused and summarily found culpable in a frenzy of injustice of murdering Chaim Arlosoroff on the beach in Tel Aviv. Arlosorff was the head of the political department of the Jewish Agency and a prominent leader of Mapai. Jabotinsky had come to Vienna to defend the accused. He said to the audience: "They are as guilty as you and I" meaning that they were not guilty at all. It was later revealed that the accusations and the trial were a despicable ploy by the Labor Movement to discredit Jabotinsky and the Revisionist Party. In subsequent investigations it was revealed that there wasn't a shred of truth to those allegations: indeed, that the crime was committed by an Arab. But it was a harbinger of the divisive tension between Mapai and the Irgun that I was caught in, forcing me to make a life-changing choice.

It was the most difficult decision of my life. How could I leave my aged parents behind? I had no brothers or sisters to look after them. However, I felt that I could do more for the State of Israel outside its borders. My subsequent years have borne this out. In my heart I was determined not to return as long as the same divisive conditions that I had experienced prevailed. At the airport in Lod, where I boarded the El Al airplane to New York, I saw my aged father through the small window of the plane, waving good-bye to me. I doubt whether he could have seen me waving back. It was the last time I saw him. I entered the United States on a visitor's visa in October of 1950.

תל חי

My Life in and Out of America

I never regretted leaving Israel after it became so divided. Partisanship split the country between the pioneers and a new group of petty bureaucrats. The events that followed my departure vindicated my decision. I knew that someday I would return, but until that time came I would have to be content with occasional visits.

My first stop after leaving Israel was in Rome where an old friend, Zvi Bar Sake the consul general, received me warmly. He did not know the circumstances prompting my decision to leave Israel. I saw him again years later when I visited Istanbul, Turkey, where he was assigned as consul general in Istanbul. Tragically, he was killed in a car accident during a visit to London.

I landed in New York at Idlewild Airport (now JFK), which had just opened. I was welcomed by the secretary of the Israeli Consulate, Martha Lowenstein, an efficient administrator, with whom I corresponded regularly. Also welcoming me was my cousin, Richard Herrup, whom I had not seen since his departure from Vienna after the

Nazi occupation of Austria. Richard arranged a hotel suite for me in the fashionable St. Moritz hotel on Central Park South, maybe knowing how much I liked the town of St. Moritz in Switzerland.

Another cousin, Ithiel Pann (Esther and Abel Pann's son) who worked in the Israeli Consulate, rented a room for me from which I had a long ride to the Israeli Consulate in the center of Manhattan. Every day I joined Abba Eban on his way to the United Nations, at that time in Lake Success, Long Island, just outside the city limits, where he was Israel's representative. It was an interesting experience to meet the U.N. delegates, among them Andrei Vishinsky, the notorious communist prosecutor; Andrei Gromyko, who had voted in favor of the resolution to establish the State of Israel; and Jacob Malik, who was the permanent representative of the Soviet Union. I had, a few years back, spent a short vacation in Tiberias at the hotel Galei Kineret, and found myself sitting on the beautiful porch next to Mrs. Paula Ben-Gurion and her friends. Mrs. Ben-Gurion was relating some quite personal stories to the other women. Suddenly, David Ben-Gurion, accompanied by his aide de camp Meir Argov, came out and called to me. He said he had a bit of a problem. Two important visitors had arrived. One of them was Serge Koussevitzsky, the illustrious conductor of the Boston Symphony Orchestra, and the other was the famous soil conservationist, Walter Clay Lowdermilk, a man whose career I had followed and whom I admired. Lodwermilk's plan was to generate power from a canal to be built connecting the Dead Sea to the Mediterranean, which intrigued me. Argov stated that Ben-Gurion would like to spend some time with Lowdermilk and asked me if I could accompany Maestro Koussevitzsky to Ein-Gev on the other side of Lake Kineret. In addition to the boat we would board, a police boat would accompany us. Accommodating the wish of the prime minister presented a conflict for me. I had always been an ardent listener to classical music and the name of Koussevitzsky was well known to me. We had, in fact, met before, and I wished to see him again.

On the other hand, I had been interested in Lowdermilk's proposal to bring the waters of the Mediterranean to the Dead Sea 1,320 feet below sea level. Construction of a hydro-electric power station on its waters would provide electricity for the Negev. I had long been fascinated by the Tennessee Valley Authority, proposed by Senator Norris and championed by FDR, and believed that a dry country such as Israel could profit by replicating the multi-purpose nature of the TVA. For a while, indeed, I thought of the application of Lowdermilk's plan as the "Jordan Valley Authority," resonant if not quite geographically accurate.

I could not refuse the request of Prime Minister Ben-Gurion and so we set out on our way to Ein-Gev. Aboard also were Mrs. Koussevitzsky and a prominent musicologist Peter Gradevitz, as well as a young conductor, a student of the maestro's. Koussevitsky to my surprise, was dressed in a beautiful black pelerine with a white scarf, white gloves, and a large black hat, the very image of a prestigious symphonic conductor. Mrs. Koussevitzky was dressed more appropriately, casually, for a visit to the kibbutz. Arriving in Ein-Gev, we were met by a group of representatives of the kibbutz, including Teddy Kollek, one of its founders. Many of the founders of Ein-Gev were my friends from Vienna. Our party was shown the bunkers where the children of the kibbutz had hidden when the Arabs shot down at them from the mountain above, called Susita. Naturally, Koussevitzsky and his wife were deeply impressed by what they saw. Before they boarded the boat to return to Tiberias, a spokesman for the kibbutz approached Koussevitzsky and told him that the community planned to build a larger music shed for the annual concerts that take place in Ein-Gev during Passover. Their spokesman confessed that they were struggling with the acoustics of the shed and asked if Koussevitsky could give him any advice. I stood next to Koussevitzsky and noticed tears coming down his cheeks. Visibly affected, he said to me, "I have never met such people. On the one hand they showed me the bunkers where the children were hiding from the Arabs in the War of Liberation, and on the other hand, they are concerned to assure acoustics in a new music shed." His response to the young men was that acoustics could not be assured in building the shed; it is a matter of luck. For example, there are excellent acoustics in Carnegie Hall in New York, while in the Avery Fisher Hall in New York's Lincoln Center, additional installations were required to assure acoustical adequacy.

On the way back to Tiberias, Koussevitzsky profusely thanked me for accompanying them to the kibbutz, and invited me to visit him in America whenever I should be there.

Shortly after my arrival in America, friends suggested

that I visit Tanglewood and attend a concert by the Boston Symphony Orchestra. Recalling our previous meetings, I contacted its conductor, Maestro Koussevitzsky, who cordially invited me to tea at his home. After listening to the wonderful concert while looking out at the lake from the veranda of their home, Seranak, a name derived from the names of Serge and Natalie Koussevitsky, I was reminded of my youth and my attendance at the Salzburg Music Festival with my mother. I believed I had now had found the best place to spend my summer vacations in my new country. Since then, I have vacationed in Lenox, Massachusetts—Tanglewood's home in the magnificent Berkshire Mountains—every year. I knew some of the conductors and soloists from Israel, among them Charles Munch, Dmitri M. Mitropoulos, Leonard Bernstein, and soloists Isaac Stern, and Alexis (Siggi) Weissenberg, a close friend from Israel.

On my return to New York City, I felt obliged to visit the secretariat of the United Nations, which had just moved into its new headquarters in Manhattan, the land on which it sits donated by the Rockefeller family. The U.N. Secretariat had previously been helpful in supplying me with printed material needed for the establishment of Israel's diplomatic delegations. My first appointment was to see Mr. Byron Price, the assistant secretary general of the United Nations. He mentioned that he was expecting my arrival and welcomed me with the utmost courtesy. He explained he was surprised to have not heard from me after he had sent an invitation to attend the inaugural conference of the United Nations Technical Assistance Administration for Training and Exchange of Views in Public Personnel Management. I now wondered why I

never received this invitation. To avoid any embarrassment to the government of Israel I explained that I was
constantly in transit and did not receive his invitation. He
advised me to report to the Technical Assistance
Administration to obtain further details on the conference. I met with an assistant secretary general of that
body, Mr. Silva, a Brazilian. In the absence of the credentials that were required from the government of Israel to
approve my delegate status, I was told that until such
time as I received those credentials I could participate in
the conference as an observer, a splendid solution.

I immediately left for Washington and arrived at the
Israeli embassy an hour before Israel's new ambassador
to the United States, my former colleague and teacher,
Abba Eban, was about to present his credentials to
President Harry Truman. I apprised Eban of my predica-
ment just before he entered the car sent by the president
to take him to the White House. Eban promised that he
would inquire directly from Prime Minister Ben-Gurion
why the United Nations invitation was not forwarded.
Meanwhile, I attended the sessions as an observer and
was even called upon to participate in the discussions. My
colleagues were chosen from among the civil service com-
missions in various countries of the world, big and small.
Among the participants were the civil service commissioners of England, France, Norway, Denmark, Canada,
the Philippines, Haiti, Puerto Rico, Uruguay, Venezuela,
Costa Rica, China, and Egypt. After initial presentations,
the delegates were asked to deliver an informative talk
about their experiences in their own countries that could
be helpful in achieving the major objective of the confer-

ence, namely the drafting of an international civil service code.

My own presentation seemed to be well received and when the conference proceeded to elect a chairman, the representative of the United States, George Vietheer, was unanimously elected. When my name was suggested for nomination as rapporteur general (essentially a recording secretary), and was brought to a vote, it received unanimous approval. Before casting his vote, the delegate of Uruguay gave a five-minute speech in Spanish rather than a simple aye or nay. It was translated into English: "the honorable delegate of Uruguay says 'yes.'" I was honored and delighted that the representative of the young country that had just come into existence was recognized by all the participating nations. I was particularly astonished that the delegate of Egypt, a country with which Israel was still in a state of war, voted for me. In earlier social gatherings before the vote, I had established a cordial relationship with the Egyptian representative. I discovered that the delegates were not required to abide by the instructions of their governments but had the prerogative of casting their vote based on their personal discretion.

The foreign delegates welcomed the initiative of the United Nations Secretariat in facilitating their visit to certain fascinating places in the United States. We toured Niagara Falls and were invited to attend a conference of civil service commissioners of the United States in Atlanta, Georgia. In Atlanta, I was invited to a Jewish home for Shabbat and was pleasantly surprised to discover this vital Jewish community in the South. While at the conference I was pleased to meet two renowned professors: Professor Herman Finer of the University of Chicago and Professor Pfifner of the University of Southern California. I also met McGeorge Bundy, the eventual National Security Advisor to the President. When I was introduced to him I made a faux pas, asking him about the functions of his department, in the grotesquely mistaken belief that he dealt with Social Security.

I maintained an office in midtown Manhattan, and settled into the life of a busy New Yorker. I continued to travel widely but also took advantage of the cultural richness New York offers. I was able to indulge my love of opera at the old Metropolitan Opera House and, as the years went by, paid frequent visits to Carnegie Hall and the new Lincoln Center.

Returning to the U.N. sessions I received a little note brought by a young female clerk in the registry there who had circulated my speeches. Charmingly, she said that she was proud to see an Israeli representative at the conference. Her name was Vera, and she invited me to visit the registry whenever convenient. Thus, we became acquaintances, and eventually good friends. She married the famous Violinist Isaac Stern at a service I was unable to attend, but I saw the Sterns often; we lived in the same building on Riverside Drive. When my father passed away, it was Vera Stern who sent the food and incidentals for the shiva. At the completion of the conference, all participants met with the Norwegian Trygve Lie, the first secretary general of the United Nations. He arranged with the Technical Assistance Administration to offer me a fellowship in public administration, in recognition of my participation at the conference, my experience as director of Personnel and Administration of the Israeli Ministry of Foreign Affairs, and previously as a founder of the Israel Institute of Public Administration. The position involved visiting twenty-eight universities around the country to survey their curricula in public administration with an eye towards how it could benefit students from underdeveloped countries. I was indeed pleased to receive this assignment, which in addition gave me another professional opportunity to see America. When I completed my survey, I submitted my recommendations to the Technical Assistance Administration. Visiting the University of California in Berkeley, I was greatly impressed by its excellent program in public administration. I met Professor Harry Fischel, a graduate of the Hebrew University who headed the Hebrew faculty at the university. We struck up a long friendship. When the Passover holidays approached, he introduced me to the Bondy family in the neighboring city of Oakland. I was invited to spend the Seder nights with the Bondys. They followed the Sephardic customs reading the Haggadah, the traditional Passover story. The university arranged for my accommodations in the International House, where I met many foreign trainees, and I was also invited to give a lecture at the Hillel Foundation on the campus.

While in Berkeley, I finally had the opportunity to meet the famous U.S. soil conservationist, Walter Lowdermilk, and was able to have dinner and chat with him at his home. Of course we spoke about my analogy of the envisioned Jordan Valley Authority/Mediterranean-Dead Sea projects with the TVA.

Before leaving Berkeley, I received a call from Harry

Beilin, the consul general of Israel in Los Angeles at the time. He asked me to take his place at a mass rally in the huge Civic Auditorium in San Francisco, and convey greetings on behalf of the government of Israel on the occasion of Israel's Independence Day. I knew that San Francisco was the headquarters of an American Jewish organization that strongly opposed the establishment of the State of Israel. Before entering the auditorium, members of a local Jewish youth organization alerted me that people unfriendly to Israel might heckle me. The San Francisco auditorium was full to capacity, 6,000 people. The stage was beautifully decorated with American and Israeli flags. Mayor Robinson of San Francisco was scheduled to address the gathering. Cognizant of the presence of that anti-Israel Jewish organization, I spent some time weighing alternative opening remarks that, this being my contentious nature, would unquestionably annoy the group. When I was called upon to speak, I began by saying, "I come to you from the Jewish State of Israel." These opening comments were greeted enthusiastically by the bulk of the audience, drowning out any nay-sayers.

Moving on to Denver to survey the program in public administration offered by the University of Colorado in Boulder, I read a notice one evening that a train would be leaving the next morning for the ski area in Winter Park. An avid skier, I decided to go, assuming that once I arrived in Winter Park I could certainly find a lodge where I could rent skis and the appropriate clothing. I boarded the train in my dark suit and homburg hat, an outfit better suited for a United Nations session than a ski trip. The passenger train included a large group of Boy

Scouts. After the train started moving, the scoutmaster, having observed my attire, inquired where in the world I was going, as he could not believe that I was planning to ski. I said I intended to rent both skis and the necessary overalls in a local ski shop upon my arrival. As far as he knew, there was no ski shop at the railway station. He warned me that I would have to stay on the train all day until it returned to Denver in the evening. I guess he really believed in the Boy Scout's motto "Be Prepared." I began to have doubts, but the train was already in motion.

Arriving in Winter Park, in the breathtaking Colorado Rockies, I was relieved to learn that indeed there was a ski shop near the station where I could rent equipment. In speaking to the owner of the ski shop, I deduced from his accent that he must be a native of my native Vienna. He was shocked when I continued our conversation in Viennese dialect. In a fraternal spirit, he rented me the outfit, and off I went to the top of the mountain to enjoy my unexpected but brief ski vacation.

When I climbed the mountain, I noticed a group of young people all dressed in sweaters with the inscription "University of Michigan." They tried to ascend the mountain straight on with their skis. Novices, they were sliding down whenever they tried to ascend in this fashion. I felt compassionate (though, as usual, puckish) and offered my services to give basic lessons in skiing. They gladly accepted, and for the next hour I showed them the elementary steps in climbing a mountain on skis. One of the students, who noticed my foreign accent, asked me what country I came from. I mischievously answered that I came from Israel, hiding my Austrian origin. In disbelief, he asked whether there was snow in Israel. Jokingly, I responded that, thanks to the Point Four program of the United States, Israel receives annually large quantities of snow, which enables Israelis to ski. He turned away, astonished, thinking what a waste of American taxpayers' money that must be.

One of the highlights of my survey of programs in public administration was my visit to Princeton University. I met the head of the economics department, who was writing a book on Israel's government administration. He asked my advice, which I gladly offered. We became friends, and I asked whether he could arrange for me to meet with Professor Albert Einstein in the Princeton University School for Advanced Studies. He obliged, whereupon I received an appointment with the great man, which his secretary, Mrs. Helen Dukas, arranged for me. While I was waiting in the lobby outside his office at the appointed time, Professor Einstein came out, took me by the hand and accompanied me to his desk. When I sat down across from him, he gestured for me to take the seat next to him. Behind his desk I saw a large blackboard inscribed with mathematical formulas that most likely he was the only person to understand. He told me that he was in the middle of research to convert matter into time, and, frankly, I did not understand a word he was saying.

Professor Einstein asked about my academic interests. I told him I was researching the possibility of establishing a Jordan Valley Authority or something comparable in Israel similar to the Tennessee Valley Authority in the United States. I explained that I had been concerned with the limited water resources in Israel, which were continuously shrinking. I thought a canal, from the Mediterranean to the Dead Sea might address the problem.

The Dead Sea lies 1320 feet below sea level making it the lowest point on earth. Explaining that, by linking the Dead Sea to the Mediterranean by a canal and using the slope of territory from the sea level of the Mediterranean to the Dead Sea, the possibility existed, in my opinion (in the presence of Einstein, a very *humble* opinion) to bring water from the Mediterranean to irrigate the southern part of Israel, the Negev. By building a hydroelectric power station midway from the Mediterranean to the Dead Sea, and harnessing the power generated, the production of electricity would further the industrialization of the Negev. I noted the main problem at that time in implementing this project was the danger of corrosion of the turbines from the salt water of the Mediterranean. I thought that the problem could be solved by a process of desalination. I further believed that the project could also be of benefit for Israel's neighboring countries. Professor Einstein, who listened attentively to my theory, briefly responded that he found the project quite feasible.

Our conversation continued with a discussion of the political situation in Israel. Just before leaving his modest office, I asked Professor Einstein if he would agree to go to Israel and become its president. I said it would certainly enhance Israel's position in the world. Professor Einstein answered that he was too preoccupied with his work, and he would not be able to go to Israel "just for the hullabaloo" it would create.

158 • DR. MORDECAI HACOHEN

The criterion guiding my investigations of the various curricula in public administration was my belief that one objective of a university was to afford students the opportunity to exchange experiences with other, disparate faculties. The policy of American universities, on the other hand, was to provide specialized training. I stubbornly felt that specialization in certain areas of public administration before completing an undergraduate training was not desirable. I understood that in order to meet the great competition in the job market in America the need for a specialization in a narrow field of public administration at the early stage of their training might be necessary. In my opinion, the programs that the Universities of Chicago, the University of California (Berkeley), and the universities of Minnesota and Texas offered were the best suited to meet the requirements in public administration of students from underdeveloped countries. My visits to Harvard, Princeton, and Yale, confirmed the validity of my perception. In this particular area, these fine universities were marginally inferior to the large state universities I cited. When I reported the findings to the U.N. and the results were made available, I was exposed to considerable criticism by the Ivy League and other eastern universities.

Since the conditions that prompted me to leave Israel had not changed in the interim, I chose to remain in America to complete my graduate and post-graduate studies. To do so, I asked the president of Columbia University in New York, Dr. Grayson Kirk, who had succeeded Dwight D. Eisenhower, to accredit me as a student and grant me permission to do my research pertaining to the Jordan Valley Authority (as I was now calling the overall project). I explained the advantages of implementing this project in the very near future to secure an ample supply of water for irrigation and industrialization to the Negev. Mr. Kirk kindly appointed me as a visiting scholar at Columbia University, which enabled me to attend any lectures of interest and afforded me the use of the of the university's extensive library.

Having resigned from government service in Israel, I now, once again, had no source of income. Looking for a job, I learned that the Jewish Agency Youth Department was in need of a coordinator for its summer programs in Israel. The Jewish Agency employed me to recruit students from American universities for participation in their summer programs: "study, work and travel." Students were to spend two weeks in Israel learning its history, two weeks at work in Jewish settlements, and two weeks of travel through the length and breadth of the country. I organized a committee of illustrious sponsors for this project including Professor Einstein, Abba Eban, and the presidents of all national Jewish organizations in the United States. I visited many universities and encouraged Jewish students to enroll in this program. Between January and July 1951, some two hundred participants from nineteen states had registered. When they left for Israel my employment with the youth department of the Jewish Agency concluded.

The Zionist Organization of America offered me a new job, directing its youth department. I accepted this assignment on a temporary basis only because I did not wish to become involved in local Zionist politics. Within the three months that I served in this position, I organized a number of social events and instituted a series of well-attended lectures. Both of these diversions attracted many Jewish students. During my stay in America, various methods of persuasion were applied to encourage my immediate return to Israel. My status as a visitor was about to expire. The only option open to me was to enroll at a university and change my status, hoping that I would be given a student's visa. The New School for Social Research in New York accepted me as a full-time graduate student. The Department of Immigration now granted a student visa of unlimited duration. I registered for the courses required for my graduate degree and simultaneously continued my research at Columbia. My professors at the New School were mostly refugees from Germany who once occupied senior government positions in the Weimar Republic and were now associated with Ivy League universities. They encouraged me to write a thesis for my masters degree on the subject of my choosing. They also suggested I write a dissertation for a doctoral degree on the same topic following my graduation. I successfully completed the requirements for both these degrees and, at the end of the torturous path, I became Doctor Hacohen. My upbringing in Vienna had created a great respect for learned authorities, whether rabbis, scholars, or professionals, and I now felt I deserved some of that. The German language's use of the term "Herr Professor . . ." has, I realize, carried over into a certain formality in my attitudes and, in fact, my English usage.

My father passed away while I was employed in the Jewish Agency. He had been a mentor as well as a good father, sharing and fostering many of my strong religious and political beliefs. His death was a heartrending blow.

While grieving, I carried on at the Jewish Agency, concerned with the recruiting of students for the summer institute. One day a striking young woman, whom I instantaneously found quite attractive, stopped by our office to invite a colleague, an emissary of Israel, to lecture at the Young Israel of Hunter College. This young lady was president of the organization there. Since my colleague did not see fit to introduce me, I introduced myself. Her name was Hoshanah Eliovson, and I inquired about the courses she was taking. She told me that she was a political science major. Politics was ingrained in her as the granddaughter of a genuine pioneer, one of the founders of Tel Aviv, although she had been born in Brooklyn.

Never in my public career had I used my position to ask for a date with a young lady. I felt that an exception to the rule was in order; indeed, I may not have thought of the "rule" at all. Hoshanah willingly gave me her telephone number. I soon asked for a rendezvous on the following Saturday evening. That night, waiting in vain for over an hour, I called her home. Her mother explained that because of the conclusion of Shabbat at the late hour at this time of the year, she was only then on her way to meet me. We spent our evening at Tavern on the Green in Central Park. During our conversation over fruit we discovered that we had many interests in common. As we were talking, a photographer approached us. I inscribed the photo for Hoshanah to the effect that this was a memorable date. I took the liberty of suggesting we would make a good match. If that came to be the case, I promised to take my new companion around the world. She did not refuse but said that she could not accept my offer in effect, a proposal on our first date. She was overwhelmed, and would require some time to think it over. It took eight months before we became engaged and decided to marry.

The date for our wedding was agreed upon with the parents of my fiancée. I then had to arrange for my mother, who remained in Israel, to come to the United States. It was not easy to obtain a visa for her. When I learned that James MacDonald (whom I met when he first arrived in Israel as ambassador) was in New York and had an office in the Empire State Building, I went to see him. MacDonald has always been what the Jewish people call a *mentsch*, a sincere and decent man. Fortunately, he remembered me from his tour of duty in Israel. I asked him to help with the State Department in arranging a visitor's visa for my mother. I could not understand why, during our conversation, he briefly went out to an adjacent room, but he soon returned with a large tray of coffee and pastries, a gracious and unexpected gesture characteristic of the man.

He promised to help, but suggested that I should first secure an affidavit assuring the American government that my mother would not become a burden to the economy of the United States. I obtained this from Dr. Henry Raphael Gold, renowned psychoanalyst and a brother of Rabbi Wolf Ze'ev Gold, a signatory on Israel's Declaration of Independence, after whom the girl's school in Jerusalem, Machon Gold, run by the Jewish Agency was named. Shortly thereafter my mother phoned from Israel to say that an officer of the American Consulate in Tel Aviv had hand delivered a visitor's visa. She was now eager to come to the United States to meet my bride-to-be, shifted into mother-of-the-groom mode and made her presence heartwarming.

I married Hoshanah Leah Eliovson, daughter of Moshe Tuvia and Shulamit Eliovson and granddaughter of founders of Tel Aviv, Yehoshua and Beelah Eliovson and of Rabbi Moshe Leib and Dina Bernstein, founders of Shaarei Chessed in Jerusalem. The wedding was austere, especially by today's standards, but very impressive nonetheless by virtue of our guests in attendance. The rabbi who married us was Rabbi Naftali Carlebach who was joined by many Torah luminaries and distinguished government and international personalities, among them Ambassador Moshe Tov who helped swing some crucial votes in the United Nation's partition decision. Customarily, there are seven blessings in a wedding ceremony. We had so many rabbis under the chuppah (the traditional wedding canopy) that to honor them all properly, I had to add additional blessings to the ceremony.

Our ceremony started inside the synagogue's sanctuary where I said the Kaddish (mourner's prayer) for my father, after which everyone went up onto a park-like roof of the 86th Street Jewish Center, which had been beautifully decorated with grass turf, small trees and hedges, and a few modest but tasteful floral bouquets. It was a beautiful day that November 1, 1953, and the beginning of a long and happy marriage that produced four wonderful children: Israel, Ariel Menachem, Naomi Malka, and Yael Pnina. In gratitude to the Almighty, we have been happily married ever since, raising a family and living a wonderful life.

Our wedding was majestic. Preparing for it, however, was quite another matter. Since the wedding was to take place at the Jewish Center in Manhattan, and I was essentially still a foreign representative of sorts, I felt obliged to invite my many friends, colleagues in the Foreign Ministry, delegates who attended the conference at the United Nations, and rabbis whom I had known since childhood. In signing an agreement with the Jewish Center, I had therefore the irksome task to make it a condition that only those rabbis and friends of my choice would be allowed to conduct the wedding ceremony. The director of the Jewish Center considerately agreed to that reasonable condition in a signed contract.

The ceremony was scheduled to be held outside the synagogue on the roof of the building under the open sky. I had arranged with gardeners to cover the entire roof with grass, turning the area, if only temporarily, into a garden. One day before the wedding the revered rabbi of the Jewish Center, phoned to say that unless he performed the ceremony, he would call the police and close the synagogue. He apparently thought that it would hurt his standing in the community if the presiding rabbi did not perform the ceremony in the presence of such distinguished guests. In tears, I pleaded with him that I had just lost my father and was planning the wedding on my own with great care. Considering my status with the government of Israel and the United Nations, I *had* to invite colleagues and the many friends who helped during my stay in the United States. I respectfully asked the rabbi to withdraw his threat and allow the ceremony to be held as planned. He finally agreed to a compromise that would allow his assistant rabbi to bless us at the wedding ceremony. It was to accommodate this new rabbi, as well as honoring my own chosen guests, that I had to add more blessings than the customary seven required in the Jewish wedding ceremony. These supplemental blessings, including one for the welfare of the State of Israel, for the welfare of United States, and for the welfare of the Jewish people everywhere, were simply woven into the fabric of the wedding. In addition to myself, since I was marrying Hoshanah, my guests were *truly* and multiply blessed.

A lavish party, befitting all the diplomats and other distinguished guests attending, followed the ceremony.

After a month-long honeymoon in Florida, Hoshanah and I bought a house in Queens, New York City, a lovely neighborhood where we have lived ever since. As I had promised, we traveled extensively throughout the United States, Canada, Europe and South Africa, where, interestingly, my father-in-law had been born.

As a child, I traveled to St. Moritz in Switzerland to ski. When my children were growing up, I enjoyed teaching them how to ski. Every winter we went St. Moritz where we kept a rented apartment. In the summer we went to Lenox to attend the concerts of the Boston Symphony Orchestra in Tanglewood. In the winter over shorter weekends we went skiing in Killington and Stowe, Vermont, or in the scenic, if less spectacular, Adirondacks and Catskills of New York State. I was becoming an American, my third nationality, and I saw more of the United States than many Americans do.

I attended daily services in the Synagogue of Rabbi Naftali Carlebach and befriended his son, Schlomo Carlebach, the famous singer-composer of both religious and popular song, a nonpareil. I made many other friends within the relatively small congregation: Joshua Pollak, with whom I attended those daily services, was a founder of the Ozar Hatorah schools in Iran and Rabbi Isaac Levy was a former member of the *Vaad Hatzalah*, the International Rescue Committee of Jews from Europe. Through Pollak's introduction, I met the international president of this organization, Isaac Shalom, a well-known leader of the Syrian Jewish community in Brooklyn and a large contributor to the United Jewish Appeal and other Jewish welfare agencies. He offered me a position as the director general of Ozar Hatorah and allocated part of his large offices on Fifth Avenue in New York to me. He was very wealthy, and because of his imports from the Far East, became known as the king of handkerchiefs.

I accepted the position with great pleasure because of my concern for the oppressed Jewish communities in the Arab countries. I was saddened to see that young people immigrating to Israel from Iraq, Iran, Syria, Yemen, Morocco and other North African countries, appeared noticeably backward. An enormous gap differentiated them from other young immigrants, especially those who came from Europe, yet I considered these youngsters to be of our same flesh and blood. Who traveled to those countries in North Africa and the Middle East to learn about their living conditions, how oppressed they were, and how much they lacked an opportunity to receive a

Jewish education? In Europe, the Jewish youth either studied in Yeshivot[11] or were members of Zionist youth organizations that adequately prepared them for their accultura-
tion in Israel by *Hachshara* (a kind of orientation program,
a component of Zionist programs in the diaspora).

To study the conditions in Morocco for the establishment of Ozar Hatorah schools, Mr. Shalom asked Rabbi
Avrohom Kalmanowitz, the Rosh Yeshivah (headmaster)
of the elite Mirrer Yeshivah to visit Morocco and report
his findings to him. Indeed, Rabbi Kalmanowitz must, as
a result of this, be regarded as one of the founders of Ozar
Hatorah in Morocco.

I accepted the challenge that Isaac Shalom offered and
regarded it as an important mission. During my twelve-year
association with the Ozar Hatorah, I contributed to the
establishment of seventy-four schools with a student population of 24,000 boys and girls in Morocco, Tunis, Syria,
Lebanon, and Iran. I also assisted in the establishment of a
teachers' training seminar in Tangiers, always believing that
training the trainers was an indispensable aspect of institu-
tional development. The responsibilities required that I visit
Iran and Morocco often. I was not afraid to visit those countries after I had acquired my American citizenship.

On one of my visits to Morocco, I invited the daughter
of Samuel Bronfman, one of the founders of the Seagram
Company, and her husband, who lived in Winnipeg,
Canada, to accompany me. Her brother, Abe Bronfman,
joined the Ozar Hatorah committee that I had established

---

11 Yeshivot: plural for yeshiva (Jewish religious schools).

in Montreal. On various visits to Canada, I was invited to speak at the synagogues in Montreal, Toronto, and Winnipeg, and over the course of time, Ozar Hatorah in Canada grew to be a sizeable organization that strongly supported our educational program in the Moslem countries. The Bronfman family have been active supporters of Jewish causes and of Israel.

In Iran, I invited Lord Nathan and his wife Lady Nathan, who was a member of the London City Council, to join me, along with Isaac Wolfson and his wife, Edith, on a visit to the Ozar Hatorah schools. Isaac Wolfson, one of the wealthiest Jews in the world, was later knighted by the Queen.

Prior to their visit, I obtained a personal letter of introduction from the mayor of the City of New York, Robert F. Wagner, Jr., to the mayor of Teheran. In anticipation of their imminent arrival, the Teheran airport was closed to other flights, and upon landing they were enthusiastically received by the principals and students of Ozar Hatorah schools. Their motorcade on the way to the school took streets lined with students. When the group arrived at the school, a reception was held in their honor. Morad Aryeh, the only Jewish member of the Iranian Parliament, hosted a large gathering in his beautiful home. The American ambassador, the president and leading members of the Iranian parliament, together with the representatives of the American Jewish Joint Distribution Committee and the notables of the Iranian Jewish community attended the reception.

At the close of that momentous visit Isaac Wolfson pledged a large contribution to the Ozar Hatorah schools. He later made a five million pounds (sterling) gift for a new hospital in London, and additional donations to Israeli hospitals. The functions I had organized were so overwhelming impressive that Isaac Wolfson effusively invited me to visit his home in London. We became good friends, and I was subsequently often a guest. I was present for the visit of Queen Mother Elizabeth to his home, thanking him for his donation to the hospital. As my friendship with Wolfson grew, I was offered the privilege to write many of his speeches in England, Israel, and the United States. My behind-the-scenes specialty in these talks were Anglo-Israeli relations and the status of Jewish education around the world.

At some time in this period, Sir Isaac Wolfson contacted me for an interesting and unusual assignment. The chief rabbi of London had retired, and Sir Isaac Wolfson, as a prominent member of the Jewish community, became quite involved in the selection of a new chief rabbi. First he was intent on Jacob Herzog but unfortunately Rabbi Herzog met with an untimely death. Sir Isaac wanted an appropriate candidate to assume the position.

I was asked to conduct the selection process in the U.S. and therefore was partially responsible for the naming of the chief rabbi of London. Three alternative candidates emerged; Rabbi Josef Soloveitchik, Rabbi Emanuel Rackman, and Rabbi Immanuel Jacobawitz. Rabbi Soloveichik said he was a *melamed* (teacher), not suited for organizational functions, activities, and responsibilities. Rabbi Rackman preferred his university presidency. After Rabbi Soloveichik and Rabbi Rackman declined, I presented Rabbi Immanuel Jacobawitz to Sir Isaac Wolfson. Upon their meeting, the rabbi was accepted and welcomed as the next chief rabbi of London.

My duties also demanded that I visit other Jewish communities in Iran, and we established schools in Isfahan, Abadan, and Shiraz. By chance, I had learned that Anna, the daughter of the late President Roosevelt, was in Shiraz with her husband, a medical doctor, who came to assist at local hospitals. I used this opportunity to invite her to a reception in her honor at our school. She accepted and was received by Rabbi Isaac Levy, the head of Ozar Hatorah in Iran and several hundred students, whom she addressed before visiting their classrooms.

Arriving in Hamadan, I was received at the airport by the leaders of the community headed by the rabbi who was dressed in a *djellabah*. They immediately brought me to the graves of Mordecai and Esther.[12] Since theirs is considered a grave of *tzaddikim* (saintly pious individuals), I, as a Cohen, was permitted to visit their burial place this time, but only after removing my shoes as required by local tradition. Looking down at their graves through a grid, I was deeply moved to honor my illustrious ancestors who liberated our people from the yoke of Ahashverosh. This biblical story (Book of Esther) is behind the Jewish festival of Purim, which takes place in the spring. One of our school principals in Teheran took me on an excursion, to the ruins of Persepolis, where I visited the house of Esther in the palace court of Ahashverosh, whose foundation and columns still stand

---

12 The hero and heroin in the Purim holiday story—read on.

today. Before leaving, I was given a souvenir; a ceramic liquor set that has been on display in my home ever since.

Mrs. Eleanor Roosevelt, the former first lady, after one of her visits to Iran, wrote in her popular syndicated daily column "My Day" lauding the educational services of Ozar Hatorah in Iran. She wrote that Ozar Hatorah, by providing education to Jewish children, who were only one segment of the population, also contributed, thereby, to the advancement of all Iranian youth. I was privileged to be invited to her apartment on Manhattan's East Side. In her letter of invitation, she set the date, which I noticed with regret fell on Shabbat. Since I could not, for reasons of religious observance, travel on that day, I wrote apologizing that I would not be able to join her. In response, she asked me to please forgive her and invited me for another day. It so happened that the new date Mrs. Roosevelt had now set fell on Passover. I wrote back once again explaining the reason why I could not accept this time either. She was so gracious, in every sense a lady, as anyone who remembers her personally could attest. She unassumingly wrote back again and generously offered another date. Finally, we agreed on a date that was mutually convenient, and I enjoyed having tea at her home.[13]

As was the case with Iran, my visits to Morocco were memorable events. The hospitality of Sephardic Jews is exemplary and greatly generous. The president of the Jewish community in Casablanca, a friend of the king and

---

[13] These simple back and forth messages, exchanged with such a magnificent personage is still in my possession, and I consider it among my most precious correspondence.

a member of his legislative council hosted a dinner for me attended by distinguished leaders of the Jewish community.

While observing the performance of the teachers, I learned that many of the students were attracted to the schools in large part because they were given breakfast and lunch daily. They came from very poor neighborhoods in the slum-like Melah of Casablanca, where large families crowded together in a single room, the children forced to sleep on the floor. Every day, the young students took some of the food they received in school and brought it to their hungry parents. When I learned these children were punished for taking their food home. I felt the need to change that practice. I remember vividly the first diplomatic reception given by the Soviet legation in Tel Aviv for Israeli leaders and members of the Foreign Ministry, when the food they had placed on the table was constantly replenished so that the guests were never made to feel that they had taken anything away. I followed this example. I ordered the principal and the teachers to replenish the food on the table so that after a certain period of time the children would not feel any regret about taking food to their parents.

One of the directors in Morocco took me on an excursion to Marrakesh. We registered in the fashionable Hotel Mamounia. When I ascended the wide staircase to the first floor, I noticed an elevator door opening. Out came a wheelchair bearing a man in a large white hat. I could not believe my eyes when I discovered that it was none other than Sir Winston Churchill. An additional surprise was my accommodation in a room only a short distance from Churchill's suite. It had a beautiful view of the Atlas

Mountains. Every night, I saw Sir Winston and Lady Churchill sitting in the dining room with their guests, the American ambassador to London and his spouse, who was an actress. From my table, I had a good view of their party. Out of curiosity, my friend and I remained in the dining room long after all the guests had left. We watched the waiters carrying trays of food and liquor to Sir Winston's table. Long after the rest of the diners had emptied out, Churchill and his guests were still at that table. Sir Winston was a garrulous man, a great speaker in both the qualitative and quantitative senses of the word. The Ozar Hatorah school in Marrakesh had over three hundred students. I thought, therefore, that it was an extraordinary opportunity to invite Sir Winston to visit the Jewish community in Marrakesh. In response to my invitation, Sir Winston politely declined, explaining that he was in Marrakesh on a short visit solely to do some painting in the desert around the city and to meet the opera singer, Maria Callas.

Due to a lack of teachers, it became necessary for Ozar Hatorah to train our own. For this purpose, I assisted Rabbi Waltner, a former head of the Yeshiva in Sunderland, England, to establish our own training seminar in Tangier. That Yeshiva was so successful that it later provided teachers for our new schools in France.

While in Morocco, I took the opportunity to see the Jewish community on the Island of Djerba, one of the remnants of the exile of Jews from Eretz Israel 2,000 years before. I felt as if I was in Jerusalem at the time when our Holy Temple stood. Their synagogue, their hospitality, and even their attire brought into memory the history and traditions of the Jews at the time. The community also administered a large building, the destination of annual pilgrimages. In addition, the modern part of Djerba, a beautiful resort town, attracted many European tourists.

In a flight from Casablanca via Fez to Tunis, I was asked by the community that Ozar Hatorah also establish schools to supplement those maintained by the Alliance Israelite Universelle, a vocational school administered by ORT and a Yeshiva run by the rabbi of Lubavitch. Following their invitation, I enthusiastically established an Ozar Hatorah school in Tunis and used the opportunity to visit the ancient historic city of Carthage with its imposing monastery.

When the Jews were expelled from Morocco in the early 1960s (following the expulsion from Egypt in 1956), many naturally immigrated to France because Morocco was a French province for so long, and they spoke French. With the large influx of Moroccan youth to France, there was a dire need for new Jewish schools to absorb them.

Unfortunately, France had a very strict and protracted process for licensing schools, typically requiring a minimum of six to seven years to obtain a permit. There was simply no time to waste going through the standard bureaucratic labyrinth. The French government had already made clear their intention to adhere to an accepted policy.

Isaac Shalom and I met in his office to discuss the problem. We agreed to not sit idly by while our Jewish brethren, displaced from their homes and the country in which they were born, found themselves in a mostly alien environment, which would either oppress them or potentially and begrudgingly assimilate them.

No lengthy discussions were necessary, as our objective was clear: new schools were needed, and there was no time to lose. Armed with a budget from Isaac Shalom, I flew to France and immediately set out to find viable locations for schools specifically geared for the new immigrants. I quickly found available accommodations for one school at the Jewish Community building in Lyons.

Lyons once had a sizeable Jewish community. During World War II, the Nazis had brutally wiped it out. A new Jewish community had sprung up there in the early 1960s composed of the refugees from North Africa.

I was confident that getting personnel to run a school would pose no difficulty. However, I had to persuade the minister of culture to issue the permit to start the new school, and to do so immediately. I approached the American ambassador, Chester Bowles, to ask for his help in getting an appointment with the French Minister of Culture, the famous author André Malraux (*Man's Fate*). Ambassador Bowles referred me to Consul General Bovy. Bovy made an appointment with the head of Malraux's staff, Monsieur Lasry, and also accompanied me to the meeting. We were graciously received in Minister Malraux's office in a palatial government building. Admittance was performed ceremonially, first by a presentation of cards, and then by a military escort to the office. The office was ornate, adorned with magnificent paintings and French tapestries, presenting a regal and intimidating setting. As we sat down in these opulent surroundings, I already sensed the answer to my request would be a resounding "no." The assistant minister, quite animatedly sympathetic to our plight, diplomatically made it clear that the ministry's policies were of great importance, and there was no way of circumventing them.

At the time, France was engaged in a confrontation with the people of Algeria, still a French colony, and its liberation organization called the OAS which was fighting in opposition to the French government. I was aware that France also was facing a rapidly rising crime rate, a growing number of gangs, and public unrest, even riots. The writing was quite literally on the wall, in the form of public graffiti. Conflict was unavoidable.

Zeroing in on the problem the minister undoubtedly faced, I took the opportunity to describe to Monsieur Lasry the strictly controlled environment and sectarian schools from which the Moroccan youth were coming. I explained how they would not fit into the French public schools. In fact, I emphasized, if they would *not* be placed in an educational framework similar to the one to which they were accustomed, they would be in danger of getting lost in the tumultuous currents and might possibly end up in the opposition OAS.

My argument achieved its goal; I got the permit almost immediately. In fact, upon my return to the hotel, I received a call from Ambassador Bowles that my request had been approved. The permit arrived a few days later, and the school was established in Lyons.

I was grateful for Consul General Bovy's support, both in helping arrange the meeting and also for his moral support at the meeting itself, but as I admitted to him later, I was a little surprised. He explained that his support for my plea came because he had previously been consul general in Casablanca. While there, he had personally witnessed my achievements and the remarkable work Ozar Hatorah was accomplishing both in building schools and in building character.

I approached Rabbi Kaplan, chief rabbi of France, and Rabbi Shili, the head of Paris' only Rabbinical College, to endorse my application to the government for a license to open a school in the French capital. I also sought the help of the American ambassador in obtaining a "contract sample" that would allow me to open such a school.

During the time I was searching for a school building, I met with Baron Alain de Rothschild to ask his assistance. Entering his bank at Rue Lafitte, close to the Hotel Ambassador where I resided, I was met by his staff, dressed in their elaborate Napoleonic uniforms, who placed my calling card on a silver tray and marched in front bringing me to the anteroom of his office. The Baron was not overly enthusiastic for the establishment of Jewish religious schools in France. He felt that such schools were likely to foster anti-Semitism. I did not share his view and told him so. Nevertheless, to demonstrate his willingness to help, he asked one of his secretaries to bring me to a large estate that he owned in the vicinity of Paris, called Laverssine. To get to that magnificent building we had to walk a long distance along the grand gravel driveway. The house was already occupied by members of the French Jewish Scouts movement *"Les esclereurs Israelites de France."* As appreciative as I was, I thought this location would be unsuitable for us and informed

Baron Rothschild accordingly. Until his death, the Baron and I remained friends, and I continued this friendship with his son, Robert, who occasionally visits my home in New York. Baron Alain, his father, had been detained by the Nazis in a concentration camp during the war and was released only after the family paid a large ransom.

Continuing my search for a suitable building in Lyons, I contacted the chief rabbi there, Rabbi Kling, and asked his permission to open a school in the building of his synagogue. Rabbi Kling, who later became the chief rabbi of Nice before immigrating to Israel, was very responsive but thought the choice of a synagogue for a school was impractical. He advised that there existed a large building in Lyons built by funds from the German restitution organization, which had beautiful classrooms that remained vacant.

Following his advice and finding that building appropriate, I met with the president of the Jewish community in Lyons, Mr. Alfred Dreyfus. Although reluctant at first, Mr. Dreyfus agreed to rent four classrooms in that building if we paid a monthly rental of $2,000 plus $1,000 for the repair of damages that the children might cause. He looked upon me as one of those crazy and unreliable Americans who would certainly not fulfill his obligation to pay the money he demanded. He certainly was mistaken. Immediately upon my return to New York, I sent him a check in advance for $36,000 representing the annual rental including the provision for repairs that he had specified. We could now have use of four classrooms in that building although I thought it was unfair for him to ask this remuneration since the building was constructed with restitution funds. I had no desire to argue the point, though. I felt it more important to enlist the students and teachers than waste time over philosophical differences. I achieved my objective in a relatively short period of time. Close to 100 children registered, and I was able to bring graduates from our teachers' seminar in Tangier.

In later years my good friend, Rabbi Solomon Sassoon from England, expanded the facilities of the school and hundreds of new students enrolled in the Ozar Hatorah school in Lyons. After my younger son Ariel's bar mitzvah in Jerusalem, I took my family on a tour through Europe and, seeing the school, they were pleased to see what I had done in Lyons.

During my stay in France, I also assisted other Jewish educational institutions in Marseilles, in southern France, and schools run by the Lubavitch movement in Paris as well as a yeshiva in Le Pin, near Paris. The leaders of the Alliance Israelite, an old French-Jewish educational institution, together with the principals of the community, were strongly opposed to my efforts. They found it superfluous that we devote half a day to Jewish education and half a day to secular education as our program called for. The Alliance Israelite Schools were always more concerned in providing a French secular education and less interested in Jewish religious educational program. On one of my visits to his study in Brooklyn, I sought out the Lubavitcher Rebbe, Rabbi Menachem Mendel Schneerson, who it turned out was distantly related to my family. These meetings usually took place in the early morning hours. I complained about the opposition of French Jewish leaders to our program allocating half the time to Jewish education. I was disappointed when the rabbi asked me whether I planned to make another French revolution by insisting on our educational program. He felt that the French Jewish community was not used to intense religious educational programs. Nevertheless, I maintained a good relationship with the rabbi, whom I met on many occasions thereafter.

Around this time I was also involved in what might have appeared to be crafty maneuvering but it was for a humanitarian cause. Mr. Alphonso Laniado was born in Aleppo, Syria and was a lifelong friend of Mr. Isaac Shalom, sharing the same native town. I was the director general of the American Society for Jewish Youth Education in the Middle East and North Africa for a number of years, from 1951 to 1966, and Mr. Shalom had been my boss. One day Mr. Shalom called me with a problem he wished me to address.

Mr. Laniado lived in Paris but visited Switzerland every year. The Swiss government gave him a visa valid for only one month each time. He kept his money, the enormous sum of $1,800,000, in a Swiss bank in Geneva. On his last visit he fell sick and had to be admitted to a hospital. When the Swiss authorities learned that he had no more than a month to live they changed his visa to permanent resident. Since he had become a Swiss "resident," when Mr. Laniado expired, the Swiss took $1,500,000 in death taxes, leaving in his account only the remaining $300,000.

Following Mr. Shalom's instructions I went to Geneva and contacted its Chief Rabbi Alexandre Safran[14] to ask

---

[14] Realizing the confusion the name may cause, I should point that this Rabbi Safran was no close relation to the Safran family I had known as a child, and that the name "Safra," referring to the banker, is also not a typo.

for his assistance. The chief rabbi referred me to Mr. Georges Brunschvig, a lawyer in Bern who happened to be related to the president of the Alliance Israelite de France in Paris. He, in turn, suggested that I contact the chairman of the Republic National Bank, Mr. Edmond Safra, who had a bank in Geneva. I followed his advice and met with Mr. Brunschvig in Bern. Mr. Brunschvig said he was unable to help and I should redirect my request to the Swiss Senate, the Nationalrat. When I asked Mr. Safra to intervene, he refused, fearing that this action would hurt his bank. So I announced from my hotel that I, as an American citizen and the director general of an American educational society, would call for a press conference, which they would realize might very well trigger an international scandal about that foul decision by the Swiss government.

By sheer coincidence, it so happened that Chief Rabbi Safran had invited Swiss Senator Fisse to speak at his synagogue on the occasion of Israel's Independence Day. Rabbi Rosen asked me to join Senator Fisse in addressing the audience. I accepted his invitation happily, and with Senator Fisse addressed a large audience in the auditorium, where I complained bitterly against the decision of the Swiss government. Senator Fisse was outraged and promised his help with the Swiss government. In fact, he did help and the resolution of the Swiss government was changed to deduct only $300,000 from Mr. Laniado's estate account, leaving the balance to be distributed in accordance with his will.

The money was then transferred to Isaac Shalom who was Mr. Laniado's executor. Mr. Shalom then opened an account with the Israel Discount Bank in New York where Mr. Steven Shalom, Isaac Shalom's younger son, was a vice president. Half a million dollars of this account was then contributed through Rabbi Abraham Shrem, an emissary of the Sephardic Yeshiva Porat Yosef in Jerusalem. He allocated the funds to the yeshiva where Rabbi Ovadia Yosef, later the Sephardic Chief Rabbi of Israel, was the Rosh Yeshivah. Another half-million dollars was then contributed to the girl's school Or Hechaim in B'nai Brak through Mr. Moshe Pardo, its founder and principal. The last half a million dollars was given through Rabbi Avrohom Kalmanowitz, the Rosh Yeshiva of Yeshivat Mir in New York, who was, in addition, a founder of the Ozar Hatorah in Morocco, and through Mr. Joe Shama, a friend of Mr. Shalom, to the Klausenburger Rebbe, Rabbi Yekutiel Yehuda Halberstam, for the establishment of a hospital in the name of Mr. Alphonso Laniado in Natanya, Israel. Today that hospital is known as the Sanz Medical Center Laniado Hospital, and is the late Mr. Laniado's valuable legacy to the welfare of the people of Israel.

THROUGH MUCH of the 1950s I performed a variety of services which, although I was no longer an Israeli government official, worked for the benefit of Israel or Israeli nationals. One of these activities on my part related to a manuscript known as the Aleppo Codex. This dated from the ninth century and was what Moses Maimonides used as the source text in writing his personal Torah scroll. It is for that reason that it is regarded as the definitive text. The synagogue in Aleppo, Syria which the Codex had been housed was torched by Arab mobs rioting following the declaration of Israeli independence in 1948, but the Codex had quietly been moved by an unnamed hero (a concerned but necessarily anonymous Jew) to a less obvious site; indeed, it was placed under a pile of clothes in the old marketplace, from which it was then smuggled into Turkey.

Fragments of the Codex in the synagogue survived the deliberately-set fire, but in some cases were badly singed. Pieces salvaged from that building found their way to various places around the globe; indeed, a single isolated page was later discovered and displayed in New York. I became involved in rescuing the main text of the Codex and returning it to Israel while others chased down the missing pieces. The fragments and the original document have since been displayed in the Shrine of the Book (where the Dead Sea scrolls also now reside) at the Israel Museum in Jerusalem. Despite the fact that I was involved only in the rescue and return of the main document to Israel, I was thanked by President Yitzhak Ben-Zvi for my help as if I were solely responsible for this service to Israel's archives.

In 1965, an Israeli secret agent working as an undercover informant in Syria, Eli Cohen, was arrested by the Syrians as a spy. He had been, in fact, an enormously successful one, having penetrated the highest echelons of Syrian leadership, rising to a level of considerable trust and respect in Syria itself. He was, sadly but inevitably, found guilty and hanged. For some time Syria refused to release the body for a proper burial. I was able to address this situation so Cohen, a hero of the ongoing Arab-Israeli Wars, would have a proper final resting place in the Jewish homeland. Ultimately, I was disappointed that Cohen's remains did not reach Israel. The massive nature of many of the tasks for which I assumed responsibility in some cases, such as this, proved to be daunting. They were Sisyphean in magnitude, and I am proud of my attempts as well as my successes.

Prior to the Six Day War, when the clouds over Israel and the Middle East became darker every day, and Egyptian President Nasser threatened to unleash a regional war, I found that the Jewish community in the United States was, as usual, largely unprepared. I felt that something must be done to awaken the worldwide community to be ready for action in the days ahead.

Together with my friends in Betar, I organized an emergency committee for Israel. As soon as the war started in June 1967, we decided to request the assistance of the United States. We asked Yehuda Hellman and Malcolm Hoenlein of the President's Conference to call an emergency meeting and mass demonstration in front of the White House with Jewish leaders from all parts of the country. The Conference of Presidents acted on this suggestion and a few days later a demonstration took place. I attended an emergency meeting of the United Jewish Appeal at the Waldorf Astoria in New York. Within one hour, $25,000,000 was raised. One leading businessman, when called to the microphone to announce his contribution, said that when he had heard in the morning about the war, he went to his office and asked his secretary to find out how much money his company had in its accounts in various New York banks. He was told that they had $450,000 in cash. He instructed the secretary to withdraw $440,000 to contribute to the United Jewish Appeal, leaving only $10,000 in his account. This typified the spirit at that fundraising meeting of the UJA.

I was standing close to the microphone while listening to a small pocket radio, and heard the announcement that the Israeli army had victoriously progressed to the Suez Canal. When I related this news to the chairman and he announced it to the assembly, the euphoria it aroused can hardly be described, and the contributions that followed increased at an unprecedented rate. The community may have been initially unprepared, but it was more than ready to help.

In an attempt to strengthen ties to the Jewish population in the States, I embarked on an extensive lecture tour. I was eager to spread the general interpretation of Israel's actions during the war as a re-establishment of certain territories as Jewish land rather than as in any way an "occupation" despite some references by biased commentators to it as "Arab" land. It was, I had to repeat over and over, a *Restoration* rather than an occupation. I was nearly obsessed with what to me was much more than an empty rhetorical dispute. Words matter.

Acting on a suggestion I had made, the Conference of Presidents of Jewish Organizations called for an emergency meeting of all the representatives of Jewish communities in the United States to be held at the Washington Hilton. Each state appointed a delegation to meet the first day with their respective Senators and Congressmen to ask for American intervention and the supply of arms to Israel. I chose, as was my prerogative, to join the delegation from

Massachusetts and met with Speaker of the House of Representatives, John McCormack. Listening to our pleas for American help, Speaker McCormack issued a statement in which he promised the assistance of the United States Congress, adding his hope that after its victory on the battlefield, Israel shall not be defeated in the field of diplomacy.

Partisan efforts by Secretary of State John Foster Dulles had a decade ago weakened this sort of resolve on America's part, and McCormack (and we) did not wish to see a repetition of that posture. McCormack handed the statement to me, and I immediately cabled its contents to Prime Minister Levi Eshkol and all members of his cabinet. American military assistance arrived soon afterwards in hourly flights. In addition to American aid, El Al mobilized its entire fleet for the delivery of huge arms shipments.

In 1973, Prime Minister Golda Meir called for an economic conference to be held in Jerusalem. I had become a member of the Board of Directors of the American-Israel Chamber of Commerce, and I thought that we Americans should attend and bring recommendations that would identify areas requiring immediate attention and determine priorities in the expansion of American-Israel trade relations and investments. This would contribute to the formulation of practical proposals for subsequent consideration by the prime minister's conference. Though a private citizen, I was compelled to advance ideas concerning the ongoing manifestations of the issues that had always absorbed me.

To that end, I organized an economic advisory council

of the Chamber that gathered at a symposium in Washington, D.C., on April 27-29, 1973. Twenty-two outstanding Israeli economists were brought together to help identify those areas of imminent apprehension, among them, finance expert and Professor Moshe Mandelbaum, then governor of the Bank of Israel, Jack Kemp, a prominent member of the United States Congress, Finance Secretary George Schultz, Professor Milton Friedman, Bibi Netanyahu, Professor Herman Branover, (an Israeli—formerly Russian—scientist), Dr. Ya'akov Ne'eman, and many other brilliant minds participated.

From inception, to dispel any misunderstanding about our intentions, I made it abundantly clear that our symposium in Washington had no intention of lecturing to the Israeli government on how to organize or reorganize its economy, but that ideas and counsel emanating from a scholarly, professional group, might be salutary. We knew that unsolicited "advice" would be justifiably unwelcome.

As far as Israel was concerned, the economic performance within the short time of its existence has proven that the state almost miraculously had managed well on its own thus far. Paradoxically, Israel had to frustrate the predictions of well-meaning experts who feared that the experiments might not survive very long and the country's economy would be doomed to failure. Some social scientists had forgotten the historic lesson that whenever presumably expert knowledge is confronted with Jewish vigor and resilience, it is the latter that prevails. An atmosphere of skepticism surrounding the early phases of

Israel's economic development had given way only slowly to a restrained optimism. Today, even experts recognize that were it not for the necessarily immense budget for the country's security and the crushing and abnormal requirements and absorption of a mass immigration on an unprecedented scale, from post-war Europe and the Islamic Middle East, Israel might have been by then largely self-sustaining at a high level of subsistence. As it happens, it was well on that path anyway.

Israel's economic achievement since the establishment of the Jewish state is generally described as spectacular and miraculous, seemingly for the lack of other superlatives. The function of the economist, however, is to scrutinize economic performance in real and quantifiable terms so as to properly evaluate whether the application of a different yardstick of measurement would lead to the same results. The economist must determine whether different policies, methods, and approaches might not have attained even more spectacular or miraculous results. American Jews, like their fellow Jews of the world, have always worked to raise these questions because, in the final analysis, Israel's achievements are not those of the Israeli people alone; they bear the imprint of a universal Jewish consciousness, solidarity, concern, pride, energy, and investment. Israel is the gross international product of an intensive and passionate Jewish vitality.

While Israel, of course, still has much to learn from the developed nations on both sides of the Atlantic, and surely had in 1973, it is not presumptuous to say that both the developed nations and the "new" ones (former colonies or revolutionary governments), may find some useful lessons in the Israeli experiment. Israel has proven that the Almighty has not given a monopoly on wisdom and knowledge to the developed nations alone. A small and less developed country can also become a center of scientific research and technological advancement.

Israel's success augurs well as an example for other nations to follow and is destined, we feel, to become a light unto the nations. Israel, with a limited area of irrigated land, can produce enough food to nourish its six million people at a high level of subsistence with an additional agricultural surplus every year. If this can be achieved through scientific research, technological application, and a pioneering zeal in a limited area, is it really necessary for the phantom of starvation to be spreading its shadow over so much land in Africa and Asia? In a world that faces the prospect of famine through the growth of demographic pressures and the relatively slow growth of food production (as is happening at the time of this writing in Darfur), in a world that is threatened with industrial strangulation by an energy problem artificially created by dark forces, in a world that is inundated by all kinds of pollution, in a world that is socially and morally afflicted by an ever-widening gap between the rich and the poor—in such a world Israel stands out as a laboratory for rapid human progress through accelerated economic development. Israel has from its origins been, after all, an experiment in the construction of a new society.

Throughout this book, I have cited examples where critics before-the-fact pooh-poohed what they imagined to be an excess of planning, or a premature initiation of a plan, and consequently often thought foolish or utopian by its disdainful critics. This had been the case with Jabotinsky's dream of a Jewish navy. The perpetuation of intensive training of mentors to secure the continuing viability of such programs dominated our thinking.

Israeli society naturally has its imperfections. These are constantly the subject of frank criticism and a quest for improvement through critical analysis and dialogue. It is out of this urge to constantly revisit and re-evaluate the potential for further improvement that I assembled Israeli and American economists in Washington. We met there to seek new ideas, find new ways and means, and learn of new methods so as to anticipate and confront tomorrow's problems. We often react to crises or seek solutions only when inescapable. In the past, all too frequently, these solutions have merely been palliatives or improvisations that provided too little or came too late to cope with new challenges. The new crises facing Israel and the free world are great and urgent. I asked who, for example, could ignore the ever-growing threat of an "energy crisis" that casts its ominous pall over Israel and the rest of the world and the interrelationship of both?

We must always remember that much of what Israel accomplished in the past and what it aspires to accomplish in the future is influenced by factors outside Israel's control. Israel can never live in isolation, but rather is tightly knit into the fabric of the world society and especially linked by millions of strings into the free world. Vibrations and tremors in the world community affect Israel because the Jewish homeland has always been geographically situated upon the crossroads of world history.

Any weakening of the position of the free world means, as a consequence, a weakening of Israel's position.

In our Washington symposium we decided to reflect on the issues in light of the then-current and anticipated economic, political, and social forces in a changing free world. We felt that if we pooled our intellectual resources and drew from the vast reservoir of our scientific manpower we should be enabled not only to continue towards the development of Israel but in no small measure to the strengthening of the free world. It is only logical to assume that if so many of our kindred were instrumental in developing a Manhattan Project, there is really no reason why they cannot find ways and means to economically harness and utilize nuclear energy for industrial use and to desalinate sea water for irrigation and hydro-electric power. Thus far the costs of implementing this latter program have been prohibitive, and have additionally been deferred because of other social and political developments, but my beliefs remain unshaken.

The recommendations that came out of the Washington conference dealt with Israel's progress in the second quarter-century of its existence, as we are now part-way through our third. Israel's sixtieth anniversary is in 2008. Far-range planning and an in-depth consideration of the components of any policy had always been instrumental in Israel's progress, as it had been the Irgun's and, for that matter, Betar's. In other words, my whole life's work grew out of these bedrock principles.

At the conclusion of this conference, my public life was nearing an end, although of course I continued to watch developments in Israel and elsewhere with a critical eye, one first honed by my reading sessions with my grandfather. I have been consulted over the years for my insight or collaboration in actions to serve Israel's interests. I left this semiretirement to organize the Jabotinsky Centennial Dinner in 1980 (see Prologue), and I continue to work out of my home, in conjunction with my dear wife and the participation of my children. I am gratified by their involvement.

I had been elected as a member of the executive committee of Herut, the Zionist Revisionist Organization New York after I had received my Ph.D. I retired from Ozar Hatorah in 1966, and joined the American Bank and Trust Company under the leadership of Saul Kagan, the bank's president (later acquired by Bank Leumi), with which I was still associated in the 1980s, largely to promote the integration of Jews into America's banking institutions. I became progressively more active with the Herut, and I regularly attended executive committee meetings, and, on the anniversary of the death of Jabotinsky, I was the principal speaker at memorial meetings and organizational meetings that involved political and economic forecasts. I was twice elected to be a delegate of Herut USA at the twenty-eighth Zionist Congress in Jerusalem in 1974 and at the thirtieth Zionist Congress in 1978. On both occasions, I addressed the plenary sessions of the Congress.

In Appendix A of this book, I will elaborate on some of the practical lessons that came out of the Washington Symposium and the experiences of those involved. I offer these with as much humility as I can summon. Do not forget; I am now an old man, one who can reflect on his life with a great degree of pride. I think these pragmatic lessons can be both valuable history, and a blueprint for developing nations to follow in a changing world. Israel's is an example they can well emulate.

THE PRECEDING account of my life encompasses my childhood in the Vienna immediately following World War I, the rising threat and eventual institutionalization of the Nazi horror, and my involvement in rescuing Jewish youth from its clutches, and our European version of an underground railroad. By way of this clandestine immigration, I was able to participate personally, as an "illegal immigrant" in the historic events that culminated in the establishment of a Jewish state, and then in the formation of the administration of the resulting nation of Israel.

I attempted in writing this book to provide a good idea of the challenges we faced prior to having our country restored to us after two thousand years of exile, and in the years following. I expect you to come away from this memoir with an enhanced appreciation of the groundwork performed, often off-stage, by people who were never famous, many not even remembered by name. I have related events about individuals whose contributions deserved to be honored and recorded, but, the nature of historical writing being what it is, would otherwise remain anonymous.

Acknowledgments

To Hoshanah, my wife of fifty-five years of happy marriage; and to our children: Israel, Ariel Menachem, Naomi Malka Weiss, and Yael Penina Wasserman.

My deepest appreciation is extended to the Nobel Prize laureate Professor Elie Wiesel, who, after hearing my story, urged me to write this book.

My warm thanks are extended to my secretaries: Lauren Kunis, Beth Gilinsky, and Batsheva Mehl.

APPENDIX A
The Lessons of Israel: A Pragmatic Assessment

THE CONSENSUS generated by the group of thinkers at the pivotal meeting in America's capital in 1973 recommended an integrated and consistent policy and program for Israel, to be reviewed by way of a five- to ten-year economic and social performance project. We urged that Israel adopt a more sophisticated method of arriving at and implementing decisions for both domestic and international growth. Israel had shown nothing short of genius in developing highly workable and rewarding policies and progress, but a performance budget, a sophisticated profit-and-loss approach, lacking until then, would serve to mitigate the sharp political divisions and cumbersome bureaucratic procedures that would otherwise have slowed Israel's progress during the years immediately ahead. It was asserted that among the prerequisites for our pre-eminent desire for peace and security, none was more important than the emergence of economic and social systems that would guarantee to citizens of Israel or, if applied there, in any country the material goods and justice to which human beings are entitled and which they will inevitably demand.

The symposium strongly proposed that Israel develop

its economy by employing already existing highly skilled and productive workers for the export of industrial products. If they did not exist in any particular sector, others could (and must) be trained. Israel ought to develop industries where the scientific and technical knowledge of its people could give the nation a competitive advantage in world trade. The learned economists felt that Israel should concentrate on the production of components rather than on complete products. Israel, having digested a huge mass of immigrants, could not now import a less-skilled labor force. Thus, Israel's built-in labor shortage guaranteed a consistently high demand for labor although wage ratios had not kept pace. Israel should exploit its strengths, including its skilled labor, augment it with intelligent and thoughtful planning such as the symposium itself represented, and carefully manage its own economic development and foreign trade.

Foreign investment in Israel was naturally discussed at length, including what it was that prospective investors should know before assessing the profitability of their investments there. It was reiterated that United States policy was firmly committed to maintaining the independence of Israel and was based on mutual interests shared by the two countries. While the fundamental conditions for support by the United States would continue to be strong, we felt that an ongoing dialogue would be beneficial, and occasional differences of opinion would not jeopardize U.S.-Israeli relations over the long haul.

All participants felt that it was their shared goal to assist Israel in achieving a stability of existence and to take advantage of the Israeli population's creativity. All discussions focused on the central theme: how to foster Israel's example as a developing economy where industry should work at capacity, where investment should flow with an ever-increasing momentum, in which agriculture should flourish with greater efficiency, and where technological education and scientific research, managerial know-how, and marketing guidance should benefit the old-new land of Eretz Israel and implicitly the world at large. Were security maintained (as such a careful plan would allow), the participants felt that if this were accomplished, they would have served as architects of the peace for which Israel has always striven.

Because the record of progress thus far had been so good, the tasks ahead for Israel would not demand drastic changes in direction or emphasis, but full resource use needed to be maintained, and economic growth optimized. An allocation of resources was needed to continue to take account of the requirements for economic balance and the fulfillment of social needs. Self-sufficiency had to be achieved through further reduction in the size of the trade gap in proportion to Israel's GNP, while defense needs for the foreseeable future would continue to have top priority. The adverse effects of excessive inflation needed to be ameliorated, partly for domestic reasons, and even more importantly to improve Israel's competitiveness in trade with the rest of the world. Prompt emphasis must be given to what is aptly called strategic economic planning by Israel, and could, incidentally, be applicable to other countries in transition. Such planning, we felt, should concentrate on achieving and maintaining a finely balanced apportionment of resource use that optimizes economic growth, makes appropriate choices among competing priorities, assures social justice, and contributes to increasing economic self-reliance.

In this process of strategic economic planning, cost-benefit analyses would necessarily be more extensively used in guiding developmental choices. The existing ad hoc approach to specialized objectives was achieving them at disproportionately large costs. Alternatives must be thought through thoroughly and regularly revisited to identify the ramifications addressed. This principle should apply to all major efforts to reduce the trade gap. The prior lack of a methodical approach was inhibiting Israel's potential.

Toward these ends, all major national economic policies—fiscal, monetary, production, and employment—needed to be integrated and reconciled in terms of their impact upon long-range and articulated quantitative goals for growth, priorities, justice, and a constant reduction in the trade gap. Such long-range goals clearly distinguishable from mere "forecasts" should be promulgated by the government for periods of five to ten years ahead, even though they would clearly require periodic revision in light of their measured effectiveness or inadequacy in relation to specific goals. There must, in other words, be *accountability*.

Toward more effective implementation of this strategic planning, we social scientists suggested establishing within the government a central agency for economic planning. Precisely how such an agency would relate to the government in general, and whether or not it should be "independent" or placed within the Ministry of

Finance or some other agency, was in our view a matter for determination by the government of Israel without the advice of outsiders. The Israeli government should, however, make strenuous efforts to intrude less, and allow more freedom of private decision in the tactical aspects of economic development, so long as those remained within the contours of the strategic plan. Once the character of the free market was more clearly manifested in practice, it should be permitted to exercise its natural effects instead of being hampered by excessive intervention and confused lines of responsibility. When the above lines of activity were developed further, consideration would be given to an improved relationship and consistency between strategic economic planning and tactical efforts in the private sector. We stressed a reduction in governmental interference in Israel, only subtly questioning the predominantly socialist approach of the Laborite administration. And the degree of centralization of administrative functions would be in their interests.

The proposed reforms and recommendations that emerged from the Washington symposium, which had been conducted at the highest intellectual level, were that the attainment of the objective of expanded trade would depend *inter alia* upon a very broad range of overall economic policies and programs in Israel; and that perhaps economists (as distinct from businessmen and trade specialists) could contribute the most by focusing attention upon their specialties in economic policies and programs. The most pressing needs-defense, the economy, and social needs—would be met in reasonably balanced proportions. The trade gap would be reduced greatly in relation to

Israel's GNP. A very strong international reserve position was maintained, and sound foundations were established for further progress.

The dichotomy drawn between strategic economic planning by the government and tactical decisions under the price system should not be taken to imply that the price system should play only a minor role in the optimum allocation of resources. In fact, one of the major purposes of strategic economic planning is to help assure that price decisions—within proper bounds—should be permitted to reflect the national value of an alternative use of various resources and also the relative usefulness of alternative products. Good pricing is good planning and vice versa. That is why the traditional government policies and so-called price policy need to be integrated and made consistent.

Additional benefits would flow from the application of our proposals. By developing cross-benefit analysis, government subsidies would be conditioned less upon profitable use by individual investors—although this incentive was needed—and more upon the ultimate objective benefit to the economy of the nation. Individual and corporate profitability was essential to economic development in a mixed economy but must always be in harmony with the national interest. The imposition of taxes, insofar as they bear upon relative private incentives, was subject to the same principles.

In this context, permitting firms to charge excessive prices at home, on the ground that it would help to "subsidize exports" might prove to be wasteful. It is not uniformly true that higher prices paid by domestic consumers were conducive to the desired results in the larger picture. The cost-benefit approach implicit in strategic economic planning was needed to provide adequate guidelines to all major subsidy policies. For example, Israel needed more investment, more know-how, and more managerial skills, and these are often found together. But when a "package deal" pays for all three together, the failure to itemize how much was being paid for each and how much each was worth and how much more one may be worth than the other could lead to a misdirected application of available resources.

Provided there was reasonable conformity with the overall perspective furnished by strategic planning, investors should not be limited to "preferred lists" of projects but instead should have considerable freedom of choice. We suggested that productivity improvement was almost always of large importance both on domestic grounds and from the international viewpoint. It would be a factor in raising living standards and Israel's greater economic viability. Advances in productivity were to be vitally important in Israel because, while unusually rapid gains were already made in this direction and were continuing, the absolute average productivity performance remained much lower in Israel than in some other advanced economies. Productivity gains depend upon investment, technological and scientific progress, improved labor skills and attitudes, and they are also stimulated by sustained full employment.

The allocation of resources and other efforts toward greater productivity were essential functions of the strategic economic planning process. A more refined distinction needed to be drawn between an improvement in productivity by sector or industry, and productivity improvement of optimum value to the economy at large. The latter depends, not only upon the rate of productivity by sector or by industry, but at least in equal degree upon the allocation of employed manpower among sectors and industries in accord with strategic economic planning. Optimum allocation of employed manpower was an even more urgent problem than the average nationwide rate of productivity gains. Some of the specifics of our analysis are summarized below.

Employment. As we were not prepared to take a position that the overall level of employment in Israel was insufficient in ratio to the potential workforce, we espoused the principle that it is unlikely that the ratio of employment to the potential workforce could ever foreseeably be "too high." A scarcity of labor is in some ways desirable in Israel; a condition where there is more work to be done than there are workers to do it is a better situation than having more workers potentially available than are actually being put to work immediately. In Israel, there always appears to be a demand for a large increase in the employment of women, with, we thought essentially, comprehensive facilities for the day care of children. We consequently recommended that government and private cooperative efforts should be expended to the training and retraining of all workers, perhaps including "research enrichment programs."

More importantly, strategic economic planning should provide attention not just to the numbers employed, but to their distribution. It is essential to optimize the use of the workforce in terms of the needs and aspirations of the economy at large. The marginal value of competing types of labor utilization requires constant scrutiny. In turn, the allocation of resources to various types and level of in-service training, we found, needed to be adjusted to the desired apportionment of the labor force. While an overall "shortage of labor" is not necessarily undesirable, it runs the risk of being a costly evil when there is a relative shortage of labor in areas of national need and a relative abundance of labor in areas of lesser importance. This is the real labor supply problem in Israel, one of distribution.

Economies of Scale. It became extremely clear that Israel should select a range of business organizations that can produce on a scale needed to compete effectively in major world markets, taking into account both the requirements of efficiency and the ability to fill large orders. We found that an improvement in this area was required. It would apply not only to a wide range of large-scale business organizations but would also call for development as it has in Japan, of agglomerations of small business groups in the major export organizations. Towards these ends, the dearth of effective middle management was a severe shortcoming in the Israeli economy. We felt that government and industry *jointly* should place more emphasis on identifying, developing, and training in accord with the pressing need. This buttressed what had always been a strong component of the organizations to which I belonged: that is, training and training the trainers

In view of the powerful impact of public policy upon the private firm, strategic economic planning was necessary to help implement the allocation of business incentives in line with vigorous recognition of the requirements toward a shift toward larger-scale firms. Also, the encouragement of direct investment, we felt, should be undertaken not solely to involve funds, but also managerial know-how and equipment.

Exports. Time forbade any attempt at our symposium to spell out, quantitatively or qualitatively, the relative opportunities for expansion of Israeli exports to various areas of the world. Such tasks, of course, were nevertheless to be continuous and urgent. The human resources available at the Prime Minister's Economic Conference a few months later would be more liable to offer guidance of a detailed nature. We felt it fitting, however, to state at that point that efforts should be persistent in identifying Israel's current and potential international competitive advantages. These might perhaps be technological rather than labor-intensive and should include services such as educational and scientific services. We recommended that more emphasis upon component parts could further the development of the domestic industry and thereby augment exports. We suggested that extensive joint efforts were required toward researching geographical market opportunities not only in the industrial countries of Western Europe, America, and Japan, but also in the less developed countries around the world.

We suggested that as long as the Suez Canal remained closed, Israel could play a major role as a trans-shipment point between Europe and the East or as a manufacturing facility for European countries exporting to the East or for Japanese companies exporting to Europe. Intensified economic feasibility studies and market research as well as actual negotiations should be carried forward. Strategic economic planning was needed to develop improved cost-benefit conclusions with respect to both exports and imports. A drastically reduced trade gap was an imperative, yet choices in domestic use between home goods and imports and in domestic production between more exports and more goods for the whole market would be critical. We might go astray in terms of optimum long-range benefits to Israel if myriad decisions were made without the guiding perspective of a long range-strategic plan that integrated objectives on the domestic and international front and weighed benefits against costs. Although an overall balance and its initial payments were vital, the nature of Israeli society would warrant considerable long-term reliance upon the aid of Jews in the Diaspora and from others. Reliance on such aid was not to be pridefully discarded in an excessive desire to achieve self-sufficiency within a limited period of time. Israel, like every new and rapidly growing country, needed to depend heavily upon foreign investments. One striking example of the need for cost-benefit analysis was the problem of "value added." There may be occasions when pride is taken in particular prestigious lines of export without realizing the true costs of the imported materials used in such exports. This can lead to counter-productive policies. As a rule of thumb in the evaluation of potential export investment decisions relating to exports, the "value added" component should generally be weighed more heavily than the total value concept. For understandable reasons many "friendly" importers of Israeli products were willing to overlook delays in delivery, and some deviations from specifications. But, to attain the needed export expansion, strict adherence to contract terms was essential and must be met. In looking at the whole picture in regard to exports and their value to Israel, the quality of export goods and export service should not be left entirely within the province of particular exporters. For even if inefficient service might be accepted by particular buyers, the leeway thus allowed could ultimately have an adverse effect upon the reputation of Israel's goods and services more generally, and even upon the products themselves. The government and the private sector should work together to anticipate and minimize bottlenecks and establish and maintain high standards of quality and performance. We believed improved corporate communications would encourage overseas investments in Israel, recommending quarterly rather than annual accounting, stockholder reports, and dividend policy announcements.

The optimum flow of foreign capital demands free egress, within proper bounds—as well as access. Investments would be greatly facilitated by more efficient financial markets on which investors can rely. These include an orderly and meaningful stock exchange with well regulated practices reflecting the true state of the market. New investment banking vehicles were needed to improve the mechanisms for issuing securities by new and established firms.

Israel cannot lightly dismiss the ominous energy problem that looms over the entire world. While Israel's own energy requirements were to be sufficiently covered for the foreseeable future, we foresaw (well ahead of other "experts" and governments) the political implications of

an oil crisis. Even if artificially created, it could be griev-
ously detrimental to Israel's international relations especially those with Europe and North America. We recommended that Israeli scientists and scientific institutes
urgently recognize the need to research alternative
sources of energy. This would eventually reduce Israel's
dependency on the oil-producing countries. We further
recommended the initiation of pilot projects designed to
test new sources of energy be given top priority. If made
economically feasible, we suggested the utilization of
nuclear energy for the utilizing of sea water for irrigation
and hydroelectric power that would yield tangible and
intangible benefits for Israel's economic development.

We foresaw that the growing industrialization of
Israel was likely to afflict the country, as it did in other
industrial states, with environmental ills. We stressed the
urgency for speedy remedial and preventive actions. The
formation of an environmental policy in Israel should be
granted priority. We recommended the establishment of a
university-level school of ecology.

Inflation and Wage-Price Profit Policies. In view of the
rate of price inflation in Israel, which at the time ran to 12
percent per year, we urged that price inflation be greatly
reduced. Price inflation has disturbing domestic consequences and intolerable effects on Israel's worldwide
competitive position. But it is an oversimplification to
regard reducing inflation as an independent economic
objective. Stable prices, wages, and profits are not ultimate goals, but rather instruments toward an allocation
of resources in accord with other objectives, including full
employment and full use of resources and their most

210 • DR. MORDECAI HACOHEN

efficient allocation. Whatever methods were employed by the government to affect trends in wages, prices and profits should exhibit an integrated approach to these three elements, and a design to maintain them in a balanced relationship, geared to the attainment of domestic and international goals. The disruptive effect of inflation could be greatly reduced through our adherence to strategic economic planning, which would also help to provide a more discriminating and effective approach to the entire task of "regulation" or "controls."

Uniformity, Certainty, and Simplification. The relative prevalence of policies and programs and the previous dearth of strategic economic planning had led to excessively random and frequent changes in policies and to an excessive reliance both domestically and internationally on ad hoc special deals. Wage, investment, exchange, and trade arrangements have acquired undue complexity, inconsistency, and, above all, needless uncertainty. These conditions were highly inimical to the flow of foreign investment in Israel as well as internally within Israel. These conditions could not be enduringly excused on the simplistic grounds that they are pragmatic. One of the first tasks of strategic economic policy would be to develop sufficient perspective to furnish much more consistency, simplicity, and assurance. From the standpoint of a potential investor, a "questionable" policy that remained firm was often more favorable than a "perfect" policy that might change overnight. Sometimes, as the saying has it: "perfect" is indeed the enemy of the merely good.

Information and Education. Overseas interest in the development of Israel was inhibited by inadequate infrastructure and education, partly because of the organized preoccupation with Israel's traditional fundraising. Raising capital was a necessity, but it came to overshadow the scrupulous attention to detail, planning, and training that I for one had always advocated. The American economic advisory council of The American-Israel Chamber of Commerce and Industry, which I had established and which was behind this great meeting, was fortified by Israeli member economists who were then asked to undertake extensive informational and educational activities in the United States. We recommended the establishment of counterparts in other countries.

Within Israel this may be an adjunct to the Central Economic Planning Agency that we proposed, a joint body of academic economists and government economists should be established. This would narrow the gap between the two groups, enrich both, and bring about a better balance between theoretical and empirical approaches.

Information given to prospective American investors should be centralized to provide authoritative guidance as to Israel's taxes, regulations, restrictions, labor relations, competition, planned facilities, and distribution concerns. Such guidance would avoid past obstacles to trade and investments due to the lack of complete and authentic information.

We urged both the government of Israel and private foundations to make financial assistance available for research on Israel's economic problems. The country's wealth in human resources amply compensated for its conspicuous lack of natural resources. The Jews have always been a people of quality more so than of quantity. Modern political Zionism was conceived by a Jewish intelligentsia who were instrumental in transforming the Zionist dream into reality. Jewish intellectuals still have much to offer so that endeavors on behalf of Israel shall be based on firm and durable foundations. These axioms and considerations motivated me to suggest to the American-Israel Chamber of Commerce and Industry the formation of an Economic Advisory Council that would assist the Chamber in a consultative capacity to further American-Israel economic relations, especially trade relations.

APPENDIX B
Awards and Honors

The Shofar Award by the National Council of Young Israel, May 2, 1965, New York

Award from the American-Israel Chamber of Commerce and Industry Inc., May 22, 1973, New York

Award from The United Jewish Appeal, Federation of Jewish Philanthropies, November 25, 1974

"Honorary Board Membership" Award from the Board of Directors of the Sephardic Home for the Aged Inc., September 5, 1974, New York

The Certificate of Merit from the Jewish Heritage Festival, September 1978, New York

Award from the National Committee of American Foreign Policy Inc. May 30, 1979, New York.

The Pillar of Torah Award by Amud Hatorah VeHaYeshiva, March 29, 1981, Forest Hills, New York

Certificate of Merit from the National Committee on American Foreign Policy Inc., September 29, 1982, New York

The President's Award from the Union of Orthodox Jewish Congregations of America, April 24, 1983, Waldorf Astoria, New York

Award from the Zionist Organization of America, December 3, 1984, Long Island, New York

The Diamond-Circle Award from the Yeshiva of Forrest Hills, 1984, New York

Award by the International Soviet Jewish Immigrant Aid Society CHAMAH, 1984, Jerusalem

The Myrtle Wreath Award by the Lower New York State Region of Hadassah, 1984, New York

The Menorah Award by Kinneret Day School, March 24, 1985, Riverdale, New York

Award from the House of Representatives, September 9, 1987, Washington D.C.

Award by Ezrath Nashim Jerusalem Memorial Health Center, September 15, 1987, New York

Award by the American Friends of Jerusalem Mental Health Center, September 15, 1987, Washington D.C.

The Distinguished Service to Torah in America and Israel Award from the Yad Benjamin Educational Center in Israel, November 12, 1989, New York

The "Care with Us" Award from the American Friends Bnei Zion Medical Center, May 23, 1993, New York

Special Citation Award from the United Jewish Appeal Federation of Jewish Philanthropies Joint Campaign, New York

Certificate of Membership for the Coalition for Desert Storm by General Alexander M. Haig Jr., USA Chairman

URKUNDE: The Honorary Member Award of the Jewish Community Council, Vienna, Austria

Certificate of Merit by The Admiral Hyman S. Rickover Foundation, Washington, D.C.

The Zot LiTiuda Award (Award of Thanks) by the Jabotinsky Foundation, Tel Aviv

Various momentos in appreciation for "Educational Services to the Children" from the Jewish communities of Iran, Morocco, Lebanon, Syria, and Tunis

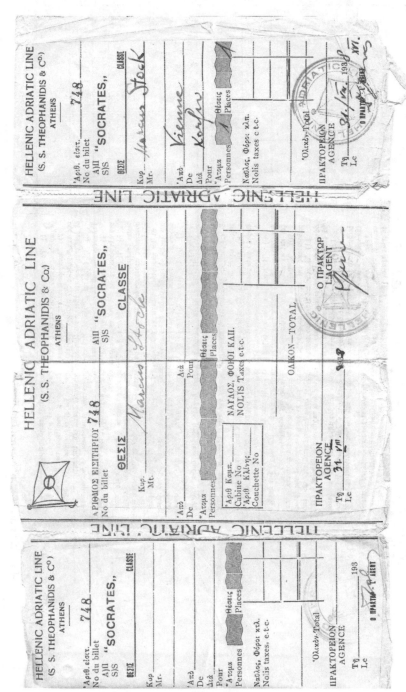

Mordecai's fake ticket for the Italian ship the *Socrates*.

Mordecai's ticket from the maiden flight of El Al.

Afterword
By Israel Hacohen

FOR YEARS I urged my father to set his life story down on paper. Based on conversations I heard between my dad and his friends and acquaintances, I felt he should write about the unique adventures and experiences of his well-lived life which otherwise would be lost to a larger public. For much of this time however, he was too engaged with other projects to take the time to do it. Fortunately, in a sense, as physical challenges began to emerge, and with an inspirational nudge from Elie Wiesel, he began writing about the episodes of his life he wanted preserved. Towards the end of his life, recording his memoirs was the project that single-mindedly kept him going strong. However, we now realize that his focus on the public side of his active life eclipsed his discussing his *private* life, his family life, and our lives together. This Afterword is an attempt to add this component.

My father was as uncompromising and loyal in his personal life as he was in his public life. The devoted concern, warmth and love he showered on his wife, Hoshanah, on his children and grandchildren were boundless and filled with humor. It set the example we strive to emulate for the next generation within our own close-knit families.

Dr. Mordecai Hacohen A"H loved classical music. Recordings of waltzes, symphonies, and marches resonated throughout our home in Queens and provided the soundtrack to our lives. Saturday nights, after the Sabbath ended, he loved leading us in song, accompanying us on his mandolin in our living room.

During the summers, Dad would drive us up to weekend concerts at Tanglewood in Lenox, Massachusetts. He would often take us backstage after the performances to meet famous soloists and conductors, such as Leonard Bernstein, who immediately recognized him. They would always greet Dad warmly, often with a hug, and forgetting everyone around them, begin to reminisce and exchange old stories and new jokes.

Dad attended musical performances as often as possible everywhere he went. He felt equally at home in Carnegie Hall, La Scala and the Vienna Musikverein. You could stop a recording and Dad would hum its continuation. He could identify the composer and the soloist whose performance was being played. Dad's facial expression as he concentrated on listening to music, or his smile as he anticipated a melody, had a spiritual quality. He had an encyclopedic knowledge of music.

My father would say, "Travel is critical to understanding the world we live in." In the course of his monumental work for Ozar HaTorah as well as for personal enjoyment, Dad visited many countries and met distinguished people around the globe. He maintained these many contacts and they would visit our home whenever they were in New York.

Dad believed travel was the best form of education and so he took our family across the United States, to Europe, and throughout Israel. When traveling, he would direct us to wherever we were going with authority. He spoke many European languages fluently and was proud of his proficiency in different dialects, which was always appreciated by the locals in the various regions we explored. His itineraries were always well planned and ambitious. Although we ended each day exhausted, we could rarely think back and find a place we would have been willing to miss.

Dad was a strong believer in helping others, which he went about modestly. When a small town rabbi in Israel wrote my father about a boy in his community who had a hole in his heart and whose prognosis for life was bleak, my father began networking to reach Dr. Christian Barnard who had just made international news by performing the first successful human heart transplant. Dr. Barnard in turn referred the case to *his* teacher who he felt was better qualified to operate and save the young man's life. Dad worked tirelessly to raise the funds and make all the arrangements so the boy and his mother could come to the United States for the surgery. On arrival here, they were guests in our home until the big day arrived. After the successful surgery, this fellow, whose parents had been concentration camp survivors, grew up to marry and have children. Another time, a member of our local community suddenly lost his father but did not have a valid passport to accompany his father's body for burial in Israel, my father was able to get clearance so he could travel and return without difficulties. I think one of my Dad's secrets was he would figure out who could help improve a situation. His genius was finding a way to reach that person and enlisting their help to get the job done.

When I was ten years old, I belonged to a Jewish Boy Scout troop and Dad participated whenever he could. He drove our Boy Scout troop to activities and would join us camping when few other fathers did. He also took us hiking, horseback riding, and boating. He enjoyed taking our family skiing in New England and to St. Moritz. Dad kept active, skiing until age seventy-seven and playing soccer with his grandsons almost to the end. He even came to show my sons' soccer teams the correct ways to pass and kick the ball.

During our childhood, his service on behalf of Ozar HaTorah, often took him away from home. Although we missed him a lot, we were proud of the example he set living his dream, working toward the betterment of our people. He made it a point to be home to celebrate every Jewish holiday and he would sit proudly at the head of the table singing famous Chassidic songs and telling stories.

When my father returned from his various travel, he would tell us captivating stories of those adventurous trips he took to the far reaches of the globe, enlisting support for the good work of Ozar HaTorah and meeting dignitaries from various countries. The gifts and "tchachkes" (knick-knacks) my father would bring home were eagerly awaited since he would present an accompanying story, sometimes funny, sometimes serious, as he would pass it around for us to examine.

Among my personal favorites was a Murano glass goblet our family occasionally used at our Passover Seder as Elijah's cup. There was also a beautiful coffee set presented to him by the Persian Jewish community. A unique replica of the King of Thailand's Barge, which my dad cleverly modified into a menorah, awed me. A small silver Kiddush cup used by Viscount Herbert Samuel on his first Shabbat in the Old City of Jerusalem, which was presented to my father by his son, Edwin Samuel, took pride of place in our home.

My father kept himself constantly informed through reading newspapers, biographies, and magazines, and by following the news on television. Dad humorously pointed out life's many ironies, yet he always faced them with optimism and determination. Occasionally, something in the news might remind Dad of a quip by the intellectual comedian Victor Borge or from the "Graf Bobby" comedy routines from Vienna and Dad would retell the joke, barely holding in his laugh until the end. Invariably, we would be swept along and laugh not necessarily because we got the joke but because Dad's hearty laugh was so infectious.

On Sundays, Dad was particularly happy. This was his day for home maintenance and other recreation. In his overalls or jeans, he would paint the fence, clean out the garage, or repair the lawn chairs. All these tasks took place before four p.m. Then it was time to clean up and dress for a dinner or social night out. Dad believed "When you go out, you should look like a Lord," or, quoting his late mother in German, "A Bugelfalte is an existenz frage." (Loosely translated, "the elegance of a well defined crease in one's slacks is a question of one's existence.")

For a time during my childhood our grandmother lived with us when she became less mobile. My father was exemplary in caring for his mother. We, the grandchildren, would bring her meals to her room daily and would sit and visit with her. His behavior of respectful compassion for his mother left indelible impressions on his children. We are a close-knit family to this day. As we, his children, set out in the world, establishing our own families and pursuing careers, Dad would phone in several times a week to discuss the current events of our lives.

Mordecai Hacohen was a singular personality-an individual with an aristocratic European charm and elegance, compassion, energy, and power. When you had his attention, you experienced a moment of great dimension and intensity. When he raised his voice to speak, all took note. All who sought his counsel left feeling hopeful, empowered, supported, and secure. He was dependable in the extreme; a safe harbor, a defender of Israel, a wise, loyal, thoughtful, and resourceful friend, a devoted husband and loving father. He was an outstanding problem solver, strategist, networker, and orator. Truly an unforgettable man.

* * *

Dr. Mordecai Hacohen passed away 23 Adar I 5768 / March 28, 2008 at St. Francis Hospital in New York just prior to the start of the Sabbath. His wife and children were at his bedside, holding his hands and softly singing the religious melodies, lullabies and songs of Betar and

Zion he so enjoyed during his life. He was laid to rest near his parents' gravesite in Har HaMenuchot Jerusalem.

The family expresses its gratitude for the vigilant and compassionate medical care provided to my father throughout his illness by Dr. Meyer Abittan. His loving kindness and encouragement, no less than his skill, extended both the quality and length of my father's life. The sincerity of his devotion gave Dad strength.

Dr. Steven Weiss, my brother-in-law, constantly tracked Dad's medical progress and offered thoughtful guidance. This reassured the rest of our family that every possible resource was considered in caring for Dad, which gave us peace of mind.

Rabbi Fabian Schonfeld, who knew my father from their youth in Vienna, was a constant source of spiritual and emotional support to our family. His sage advice guided us with strength and fortitude through the difficult times. His vast knowledge of Jewish law helped us navigate through the intricacies of traditional Torah Judaism as it related to medical ethics concerning the frail and elderly. He was and is a true source of comfort to our family.

At his funeral service in New York, Dr. Mordecai Hacohen was eulogized by Rabbi Schonfeld, who reminisced about their youth in Vienna. He poignantly related how Mordecai fought for the State of Israel and the Jewish people and now, his final journey and mission was to return and be laid to rest in the land he loved so much.

Rabbi Jacob Rubenstein A"H recited traditional psalms followed by Rabbi Shlomo Lobenstein, a neighbor and friend whose visits raised my father's spirits in his final months. Mrs. Beth Galinsky Spiro, who assisted my father in preparing the original draft of his life story, recounted episodes of courage and leadership when Dr. Hacohen championed just but unfashionable causes and individuals in need. Finally his sons, Israel and Ariel and his nephew Moshe Tuvia Elad Eliovson, added some personal reflections on his accomplished life.

Dr. Mordecai Hacohen's final journey was with his family accompanying him to his burial in Israel. Notices in Israeli newspapers led to an outpouring of mourners who joined the funeral and visited our family in Israel during the period of mourning.

Graveside eulogies were delivered by former Israeli Supreme Court Justice Yaacov Turkel, a close relative who remembered his cousin's youth in Vienna; journalist and author Shlomo Nakdimon spoke about Dr. Hacohen's vision and resourcefulness during the war years and the important role he played in the formation of the Government of Israel; Former Governor of the Bank of Israel, Moshe Mandelbaum, described Dr. Hacohen's tireless efforts in assembling symposia and mobilizing creative intellectual giants to address Israel's critical policy needs.

Jac Friedgut, a former Citibank executive and activist for Israel recalled Dr. Hacohen's initiatives as an advocate in Washington during and following the Six-Day War. Meir David Weiss, the eldest grandson, concluded the service with psalms and by sharing reflections about his grandfather. The ceremony was dignified and moving, a fitting tribute to one who gave so much of himself for others.

We acknowledge the support of Dr. Bernard Lander,

founder of Touro College and Dr. Hacohen's life long friend, for his great help in the preparation of the memoirs.

With a sense of profound gratitude we thank Mark Levine for his skillful editing of the manuscript. Mark did a masterful job clarifying the flow of the narrative while preserving the author's style.

Although my father did not live to see his book in print, he did review the finished manuscript and selected the photographs for inclusion in his book. After Dad passed away, his wife Hoshanah, son Ariel and daughter Yael (Hacohen) Wasserman scanned and captioned the pictures. Son-in-law Neil Wasserman, daughter Naomi (Hacohen) Weiss, my wife Sandi Lipshitz Hacohen and I collaborated to prepare this Afterword. Dad's abiding presence keeps the family working together.

Eric Kampmann of Beaufort Books successfully led the search for a title for the memoir. Margot Atwell patiently shepherded the project to completion. Erin Smith's cheerful guidance and thoughtful support are greatly appreciated. Our family is very grateful to them for their unflagging efforts in professionally stewarding this project to its successful publication.

Index